Think Twice

a learner's guide to improved emotional intelligence

Michael Cornwall, PhD, LPCC, CSW
Introduction from Jon K. Reid, PhD, LPC-S, NCC

Think Twice

A Learner's Guide to Improved Emotional Intelligence

Michael Cornwall, PhD, LPCC, CSW

Introduction from Jon K. Reid, PhD, LPC-S, NCC

Copyright © 2011 by Michael Cornwall. All rights reserved.

ISBN-13: 9781468084245

ISBN-10: 1468084240

Illustrations copyright © 2011 Michael Cornwall.

No part of this publication may be reproduced, stored in a retrieval system or transmitted in any form or by any means, electronic, mechanical, photocopying, recording, scanning or otherwise, except as permitted under Sections 107 or 108 of the 1976 United States Copyright Act, without either the prior written permission of Michael Cornwall. Requests to Michael Cornwall for permission should be addressed to the Michael Cornwall, 1001 Windsor Drive, Shelbyville, KY 40065 (859) 321-4956, email: michael.cornwall@eitheory.com

Please visit http://www.eitheory.com to enhance your reading experience.

Limit of Liability/Disclaimer of Warranty: While the author has used his best efforts in preparing this book, he makes no representations or warranties with respect to the accuracy or completeness of the contents of this book and specifically disclaims any implied warranties of merchantability or fitness for a particular purpose. No warranty may be created or extended by sales representatives or written sales materials. The advice and strategies contained herein may not be suitable for your situation. You should consult with a professional where appropriate. The author shall not be liable for any loss of profit or any other commercial damages, including but not limited to special, incidental, consequential, or other damages.

Dedication

Over the course of writing this book, I had the opportunity to build my emotional intelligence (EI), using articulated thought to an extent I never knew was even possible. I am convinced that a combination of tremendous adversity and increased frustration tolerance are the best environment for significantly improved EI. Suggesting that it is healthier to put up with what you thought you could not endure, if for no other reason than to find out that you can endure nearly anything, is the most effective advice I have ever given myself.

My warmest and most sincere appreciation goes to *Jill Wilson Hunter*, for teaching me people truly can be all I imagined they could be. Your positive, forward-thinking outlook in nearly any situation is a testament to the possibilities of emotional intelligence theory. I would also like to recognize the contributions made to my emotional intelligence by Nelson Bottoms, Dr. Raymond DiGiuseppe (who told me in 1992 to go out and write a book), Dr. Debbie Joffe Ellis, Dr. Thomas Badgett (whose sincere expression of his faith is neither threatening nor alienating), Stuart Owen (for whom I am eternally grateful), Gareth Coote, Nathan Stirling, Wanda Fowler, Julie *Retro Girl* Lawson, Northcentral University, Angela Hockensmith (who contributes every day to my goal of **hap-i-licious-ness**), nutty people, Sandra *Nanny* Flannery, Stacia Berry, Ellenore Callan, left-wing Republicans, Lillian McGrath, Log Cabin Republicans, Dawn Weyman, Barrack Obama, my daughter Kylie Weyman, Christian conservatives, Adam Hensley, Wayne Frazier, George Bush, Dr. Jon K. Reid, *Jenn, Betty* and *Renaldo* and, of course, Dr. Albert Ellis (September 27, 1913 – July 24, 2007), without whose influence on my emotional education and my life nothing is or would ever have been possible.

Personal Reflection Disclaimer

My primary obligation is to respect the integrity and promote the welfare of all individuals, families and groups. When discussing particular individuals and my experiences with them, I must take precautions to protect them from any harm resulting from that discussion. Unless agreed upon by a party, I have taken every precaution to disguise the identity of the individuals discussed in this manuscript. Any data derived from a learner relationship and used in this manuscript has been disguised so that that the informed learner's identity is fully protected. Any data which could not or was not disguised was authorized by the individual's informed and un-coerced consent. No notes, test data, correspondence, audio or visual tape recordings, electronic data storage or other documents were used to recollect any of the data related herein.

"There is no ability to sing; only the ability to approve or disapprove of singing."

Foreword

A positive social problem solving (SPS) orientation e.g., solution-focused, progressive, forward-looking and reasoned problem-solving strategies is believed to produce optimistic, useful emotional outcomes. Less functional SPS, e.g., ***impulsivity, carelessness*** and ***avoidance of personal responsibility for one's emotions*** are believed to be associated with maladaptive behavior and psychological distress.

Emotional intelligence (EI) theory may be best understood as a multidimensional system of SPS requiring a full appreciation for the benefits of positive social problem-solving, using a ***bio-psycho-social model*** of broad-spectrum healthcare:

- The ***biological element*** of the ***bio***-psycho-social model is allied with the oft-overlooked neuro-biologic influence on emotion, e.g., the limbic system (neighborhood), sympathetic and parasympathetic nervous systems, major organs, neurons and hormones, etc.

- The *psychological* factor emphasized in the bio-*psycho*-social model is derived (in this particular analysis) from rational emotive behavior theory [REBT]. REBT endorses the application of *rationality* in personal decision-making, often citing Epictetus as its maxim, *What disturbs peoples' minds is not events but their judgments on events.* The term *irrational* may be defined as dysfunctional thought processing that includes **exaggeration, oversimplification, overgeneralization, illogic, unproven assumptions, faulty deductions,** and **absolutistic notions.**
- The *social* aspect of the bio-psycho-*social* model is related to the unique environments in which people are reared, i.e., family, community, state, country, etc. environments that really influence thought and encourage conformity in individual and group emotional behavior.

EI theory places substantial weight on **self-efficacy**, determination and increased frustration tolerance. Consideration of each of these individual components in the administration of all forms of healthcare services, especially emotional intelligence training, may result in expansion of improvement in:

- *perception* of emotional stimuli,
- *problem-solution skills* (process methods) and
- *behavioral performance*, resulting in more competent SPS, improved EI and improvement in physical health.

EI theory highlights the role **human anatomy** and **social environment** play in the promotion of emotional behavior. Proper attention to the individual as a system of synchronized parts may result in an efficient, flexible, open-minded method for addressing emotional improvement. An EI / SPS practice lacking balanced emphasis in any of these three dimensions may result in deficit SPS competence and weakened EI. For example, if the REBT paradigm is stressed over the biological/social influence on emotional health, imbalance (rather than benefit) may result. Simply being adept at untangling cognitive mysteries using REBT is likely to result in little more than *intellectual insight* and limit overall EI achievement.

Few researchers agree on the most appropriate techniques for achieving SPS / EI proficiency. Many are in agreement that optimal SPS can be reached by focusing the learner on four integral components of emotional learning: 1) input, or the *act of perceiving and understanding the problem*; 2) processing, or the generation of *alternatives* and *selecting solutions*; 3) output, or *the act of planning and implementing solutions*; and 4) review, or the process of *evaluating solutions or modifying them, if necessary*. The steps outlined in this book are ideal for use with this paradigm.

EI theory incorporates emotive and *behavioral* (articulated thought) measures to encourage the learner to independently act against self-defeating thoughts and behaviors. By expressing a more *internally-focused* base of emotional control, and staying well-focused during the process of problem identification and problem resolution, improvement in EI is believed more likely.

Articulated thought (AT) (talking out loud to oneself rather than thinking-through emotional distress) is designed to give strength to the oft-overlooked *behavioral* dynamic of emotional skill-building. AT depends on eliciting cognitive feedback, in real-time, when a thought is believed to be *on-line*. The learner is encouraged to *verbalize* – to articulate thought, using the prompts discussed in the EI problem-solving methods found in *Go Suck a Lemon*.

EI with AT is believed to hold the promise of ordering the typically **unordered voice** of the mind. It is believed that the use of AT may enable an individual to more closely examine the questions, concerns and feelings s/he experiences when exposed to stimuli – to stay completely focused on problem-solving. Articulating one's thoughts may potentially result in fewer confabulations in thinking, daydreaming, inattention and distractions that are inherent to thinking, alone. The practice of AT is not only a vital part of the EI paradigm but can result, as well, in a higher degree of self-efficacy.

EI theory that depends solely on *thinking*, and does not include a dynamic behavioral component such as AT, is more likely to provide the learner with intellectual, rather than emotional insight, e.g., learners who acquire the knowledge base for EI's formulaic method may not be benefiting emotionally from the knowledge. If an EI learner can demonstrate proficiency in the principles of EI theory (both through **intellectual** and **behavioral** insight), s/he may be better prepared to practice the model.

From my experience, the learner who only manages to *identify faulty thinking* and does not commit to continue the problem-solving process – toward discovering a more reasonable, manageable belief option – may be at continued disadvantage for improving h/er emotional intelligence. The learner may be challenged a great deal of the time with using h/er new social problem solving skill and returning to a more familiar pattern of SPS. The learner must recognize these pitfalls and strive to overcome them.

According to the basic premise of EI theory, in order to overcome emotional conflict, we must practice and strengthen more ***useful and adaptive social problem-solving behaviors***. By establishing personal practice methods, those behaviors the learner can sustain over time, for example, behaviors that encourage *objectivity* when being judged by others, may:

- help the learner rely more on h/er own judgment of h/erself and h/er worth;
- discourage ***emotional conformity***
- encourage ***emotional range***;
- encourage ***self-determination***;
- help to build the value of ***self acceptance*** over the concept of self esteem;
- strengthen the process of ***solving one's own emotional problems***, likely resulting in ***better preparation*** for the next time shit happens.

Without some vigorous, consistent effort on the learner's part to ***think*** and ***behave*** differently, success with EI theory will be extraordinarily limited.

Finally, the most promising benefit of using the emotional intelligence theory in social problem solving with articulated disputation is the potential for the learner to recognize the similarities between h/er past and current emotional issues. If the learner is successful at ***mindful commitment*** to resolving h/er emotional concerns using this EI paradigm, s/he is more likely to use the solutions acquired from these experiences to address future problems.

Michael Cornwall, PhD, LPCC, CSW

"People are not disturbed by things; only their view of things."

Introduction

  I am pleased and honored to both introduce and recommend Dr. Michael Cornwall's book *Think Twice*: A Learner's Guide to Improved Emotional Intelligence.

  Have you found yourself feeling stuck, unable to accomplish your goals or even to set goals for yourself? As both a professor of mental health counseling and a licensed counselor, I've listened to students and clients express frustration with their inability to overcome barriers to achieving their goals; or expressing a general frustration with their life; so often placing blame on others or if not taking a blaming stance, perhaps just remaining stuck in their self-perceived helplessness. Dr. Cornwall offers a clear strategy to getting unstuck and increasing one's emotional intelligence (EI) while facing and resolving life's difficulties.

  How often have you been advised by a mental health professional to talk to yourself; even out loud? Dr. Cornwall does just that, using both humor and a penchant for cajoling the reader to *think twice*, examine one's self-talk, and to live more freely. Fear not that huge rapid changes are required, but merely changes made in incremental steps toward one's self-chosen goals.

Using straightforward steps, *Think Twice* offers emotional tools for managing one's emotions; the learner becomes a manager of their emotions, experimenting with more effective strategies than previously used and learning from the process. The outcome is a human being who more effectively faces life's challenges. Rather than becoming overwhelmed with these challenges, they possess more effective emotional tools with which to face them.

Providing tools for parents, teachers, counselors and other humans, Dr. Cornwall offers practical strategies, some newly created terminology and well-articulated analogies to make his points.

Dr. Cornwall concludes this text with dialogue from counseling sessions to show how his theory can be applied in professional settings.

To a wide audience of readers, I say: Be prepared to learn some newly created terms, enjoy Dr. Cornwall's sense of humor, and above all to accept the challenge to move out of life's ruts and *think twice* toward a better life!

Jon K. Reid, PhD, LPC-S, NCC, Fellow in Thanatology (ADEC)
Professor of Clinical Mental Health Counseling
Southeastern Oklahoma State University
Durant, Oklahoma

INDEX

COPYRIGHT 4

DEDICATION I

PERSONAL REFLECTION DISCLAIMER II

FOREWORD III

Introduction ix

ONE – *YOU SHOULD BE COMMITTED!* 1

TWO – *IT* 18

THREE – *I'M WIRED!* 35

FOUR – *I PLAY THE BITCH ROLE* 54

FIVE – *WHERE ARE MY EMOTIONS?* 63

SIX – *YOUR EMOTIONAL NEIGHBORHOOD* 76

SEVEN – *WHAT IN THE HELL WAS I THINKING?* 84

EIGHT – *THE BURDEN OF CHANGE IS ON YOU* 95

NINE: *PEACH ICE CREAM* 98

TEN – *THE DANGERS OF SELF-ESTEEM* 107

ELEVEN – *EMOTIONAL MEMORY* 111

TWELVE – *SELF TALK AND PREPARATION* 115

THIRTEEN – *EMOTION BEGINS AS THOUGHT* 118

FOURTEEN – *THINK TWICE* 130

FIFTEEN – *I WASN'T RAISED LIKE THAT!* 140

CONCLUSION 148

Sample Sessions 155

THE CASE OF ELLIOT 160

SANDY'S CASE 175

EI THEORY MODEL AT A GLANCE 179

BIBLIOGRAPHY 181

*"The traditional **therapist**, from my limited estimation, is more likely to simply keep h/er client company while the client's emotional problems run their course."*

One – *You should be committed!*

If you've ever read any of my earlier publications, you may have noticed that I often write in short blips, one-word sentences, three-word paragraphs – like brain waves, or a traffic signal that must, by its abbreviation, create an immediate impression. Frankly, although I wish I had all the time in the world to discuss the minute intricacies of *emotional intelligence using articulated disputation* with you, my learner might just want to go on and get on with it.

And I appreciate that.

I wish more of us wanted to be more emotionally intelligent as soon as possible!

If you're like most people, however, you simply want the facts about emotional intelligence. You want to know what to do, how to do it, when to practice it, how often and how long it will take until you see improvement.

Somewhat like starting an exercise and eating plan.

As you will soon discover, the analogy is quite appropriate.

Like exercise and eating right, endeavoring to improve one's emotional intelligence can result in emotionally healthy living. In fact, if you're emotionally healthy, you may be more capable of tackling those other goals you've left unachieved for one reason or another.

Many very well-intentioned people compromise their goals one little bit at a time – until the goal is only a distant memory. Goals, generally, are left unachieved because we make **one compromise after another**, until we're back to where we started.

Sometimes even further back than that.

Chalk it up to yet another failed attempt.

"I'll start over when I am in a better frame of mind."

Improving emotional intelligence will be like starting and either sticking to or compromising an excise and healthier eating plan. Improvement will take long-term commitment, dedication to practice, personal sacrifice and higher frustration tolerance to achieve. If you need to be in a better frame of mind to pursue your goal of improved EI, you won't be. You'll probably be in the same frame of mind you're in right now for the rest of your life, unless you take steps to do something about it. It is best to stay focused on improvement, in spite of your frame of mind. Actually, a shitty frame of mind is what you *need* to begin a goal of improved emotional intelligence.

****

Thinking differently about adversity has always been the tough part of improving one's emotional intelligence (EI), especially in the midst of a crisis. Our goal as EI learners, however, is to think twice – maybe not in the midst of a crisis, but at some point soon after.

The suggestion that we will have to learn to think twice implies that we will expend at least that much more effort than we do now to solve our emotional problems. EI learners know that when A happens, we often think B and feel C; just like we always have. Very little will ever change in that regard. But what EI learners know, as well, is that our options at C are not limited to our first thoughts and consequent emotional response. We learn to think differently at B and feel a new C – an evolved emotional response.

****

I now know that maneuvering through the world of feelings, and trying to convey to others the often-confusing (and conflicting) philosophies related to emotion, is best achieved using as little lingo as possible. What lingo I do use, I like to make less complicated – more pedestrian; more consumable by the consumer. I am also now very careful not to take myself so seriously and to add a bit of humor to what I am teaching. (Nothing is funnier, and more beneficial, than when we can laugh at ourselves.) After all, EI education is not about how crafty and illusive your guide can be while trying to help you improve your EI.

Neither is it intended to be a comedy show.

It's a balance.

****

Theories of emotional intelligence abound.

I have seen and heard a lot about something called ***Emotional Intelligence Quotient*** (EQ). Of course, this book discusses ***Emotional Intelligence Theory*** (EI) and rejects the idea that there is a method for establishing a quotient that is relevant to emotional intelligence. Like EQ, EI depends on a personal commitment to change. Commitment to change begins with the realization that you have had enough of the way you handle your emotional life and you want to do something about it.

So, if we are going to gauge our emotional intelligence, it may be a simple matter of **having had enough**, or **continuing to have what you've always had**.

It appears that EQ promotes *thinking like* other people. Essentially, EQ supports magical, nutty thinking and encourages an external locus of control. The person practicing EQ imagines s/he knows what is going on in the minds of others. For example, if someone is behaving disrespectfully toward you, EQ endorses the following problem-solving strategy: ***S/he must be having a bad day. I think I will just be nice to h/er and treat h/er as if I know that h/er life isn't working out well at the moment***.

Where EQ would have you imagine what is going on in the minds of others, a process of ***managing*** and ***coping*** with emotion, EI supports the idea that managing and coping with our emotions does nothing to produce long-term results.

Managing and coping are processes of postponing or even avoiding emotional improvement.

So, instead of imagining what the life of a stranger must be like, EI teaches that ***you can only know your own mind***. Instead of managing and coping with your anger, rage and anxiety, EI problem-solving works with concrete facts and long-lasting solutions: *This person is behaving disrespectfully toward me. When I am treated disrespectfully I tell myself I cannot stand it. I tell myself that it is awful when I am treated with disrespect. I tell myself that when I am disrespected, I am worthless. If I am treated as if I am worthless, people might think I am worthless. If people don't value me, I am a failure. If I am treated as a failure, I wouldn't be able to stand that. I have to have the respect and admiration of everyone I meet. Everyone* must celebrate the wonder of being me, or I am not as wonderful as I thought I was.

Of course, confronting our self-defeating beliefs is not as pleasing and agreeable as imagining that everyone is simply having a bad day. Your thoughts send messages to your body that activate a neuro-psycho-anatomical response that, once started, is nearly impossible to impede – without some effort on your part to halt it. Confronting our own thoughts and making sense of them can actually lead to de-activating your body's *fight-flight-or-freeze* response to noxious behavior, resulting in better health and continued wellness. EI does not encourage learners to *manage* or *cope* with emotion by postponing or even avoiding noxious external emotional stimuli.

Learners are encouraged to turn inward, to their own thoughts and behaviors in order to make long-lasting, durable emotional improvement.

In order to regain peace and balance, like EQ, the EI learner will have to *think differently*. The EI learner is encouraged to think in terms of *rationality* and *level-headedness, truth, fact* and *verity*. Using EI, you actively participate in the process of problem-solving by asking yourself a series of rational questions: *Is it true that I am worthless because people treat me that way? Can I accept myself and my human value even when others don't? Do I have to be thought of by others as perfect in order to live my life happily?* This process of thinking will result in a de-escalation of your fight or flight response. *No, I don't need these behaviors from others to be content with myself. I would like people to behave differently, but sometimes they don't and I can certainly stand it.*

EI takes a bio-psycho-social perspective on mental health awareness. Treating the whole person is expected to result in a more comprehensive, durable emotional wellness. It is believed that a heightened attentiveness to one's biological response to thought will provide an individual with valuable information for emotional problem solving.

It will take the force of will to do this.

****

Stress is a term that was first used in a biological / psychological context in the 1930s and continues to this day to be a common and easily recognized, yet widely misused term.

The term ***stress*** was borrowed from the field of physics and engineering. As a biological and psychological expression, the broader meaning of stress was adopted to explain the body's response to added demand - much like the considerations given to a structure and its capacity to withstand both routine and extreme conditions. Like predicting the endurance of a bridge spanning a small creek or a wide body of water, human psychological and biological stressors can cover a wide variety of phenomena, from mild irritation to overwhelming breakdown.

The phrase ***stress limit*** might reference the extent to which an organism is capable of effectively acting upon real or imagined mental, emotional or physical challenges. You may have noticed that nearly everyone you know has a unique stress limit. Of course there is an average and expected human stress response to most harmful stimuli, i.e., snakes, polar bears, hungry lions. But there are often those psychological stressors that are not immediately life-threatening that are more or less endured or suffered depending on the individual experiencing them. Some, for example, may experience *disrespect* with great fortitude and endurance, while others may perceive *disrespect* as a greater threat to life and limb and respond in quite the opposite. For example, I was watching a reality TV program yesterday where two women met at a wedding wearing the same, very unique Spandex mini-dress. They both immediately attacked one another, causing a disturbance that resulted in them throwing chairs and pulling out each other's hair. When asked to explain their behavior, she said she had been *disrespected*. Apparently, her response to *disrespect* was to tear the hair from another person's head. I, on the other hand, experienced disrespect last week. My response was to find fault in the other person.

Emotion is a product of thinking.

Change your thinking and you will change your emotional response.

Psychological stressors are often dependent upon *perception* and *interpretation* of threatening phenomena. Perception (or thought) activates the *autonomic nervous system*.

The *parasympathetic response* of the autonomic nervous system may be described as feeling a sense of rest and peace. The *sympathetic nervous system*, on the other hand, often referred to as the *stress* or *fight-flight-or-freeze response*, depends on the perception (the stimulus that causes stress) of threat and danger. Like the women in the matching Spandex mini dresses, if the human organism perceives threat, the autonomic nervous system prompts the sympathetic nervous response and releases neurochemicals and stress hormones into the bloodstream, including adrenaline and cortisol, activating the body's emergency protection response.

It really doesn't matter if the threat is real, perceived or imagined. The body will respond to its own understanding of threat in its own unique way – in the unique way you teach it to respond. They key to improved EI is to teach your mind to perceive, imagine or experience adversity differently.

There are *three phases* of the stress response.

Alarm. When and individual perceives threat the body will enter a state of alarm. During this stage, adrenaline will be produced in order to bring about the stress or fight-or-flight response. There is also some activation of the HPA axis, producing cortisol. If reasonable means of addressing the stressors are found after entering this stage, the stress will subside. This stage may be described as *episodic stress* and may be short-lived. For example, if you are driving and have a tussle with a fellow motorist, your stress level may increase. Ten minutes after resolving your differences, however, you will return to balance and hardly remember the disagreement.

Resistance. If the stressors persist, it may become necessary to attempt some means of coping with the stress. Although the body begins to try to adapt to the strains or demands of the environment, the body cannot keep this up indefinitely, so its resources are gradually depleted. This stage may be described as long-term stress and normally requires active intervention to alleviate. For example, if you receive a poor rating on your employee evaluation, and you believe you have been irreparably harmed, you may experience a longer, more protracted period of stress.

Exhaustion. At this point, all of the body's protective and defensive resources – chemical messengers released into the bloodstream, i.e., adrenaline (epinephrine), histamines that, over time can become depleted, leaving the body unable to maintain normal function. If stage three is extended, long-term damage to the body's immune system as well as other illnesses including ulcers, depression, diabetes, trouble with the digestive system, or even cardiovascular problems, along with other mental illnesses may result. If you find yourself going to bed with thoughts of failure, anger, rage or fear related to some real or imagined event in your life, night after night, waking (if you were able to sleep at all) in the morning with the same thoughts, having the same ideas all day and into the night, you may be in this stage of the stress response.

****

The term *stress* may be misused – a word used to identify the external perception of the stressors rather that the internal mechanism that controls it. Identification of the *true source of stress* is essential to doing something to about it.

The *true source of stress* is not that you are being disrespected, underappreciated, ill-treated or ignored. In the absence of a polar bear, a wild goat or a rabid prairie dog, the source of your stress is in *your own thinking*. You will not likely reduce your stress until you take control of your thoughts.

"IT is very stressful!"

"SHE is making me stressed!"

"THIS is too stressful for me!"

"I can't meet this deadline. IT'S going to kill me! I am sure to FAIL!"

These perceptions and thoughts can result in making a person more vulnerable to stressful exhaustion. It may be true that stressors that threaten one's physical safety, such as those stressors that result from exposure to wild animals and poisonous spiders, psychological stress is more often a result of one's own thinking and perceiving.

The kind of stress found in modern life is often psychological and can be better addressed through education. Learning to think and perceive differently can go a long way to reducing one's experiences with stress. Recognizing that no one makes you stressed other than you and your own thoughts may result in avoiding long-term exposure to the noxious hormones that will likely result in mental and physical breakdown.

It will take the force of will to do this.

****

Your thoughts send messages to your body that activate a neuro-psycho-anatomical response that, once started, is nearly impossible to impede - without you taking some active role in halting it.

In order to regain peace and balance, like EQ, you will have to **think differently**. Only with EI you are thinking in terms of rationality and level-headedness, truth, fact and verity. Using EI, you are expected to actively participate in the process of problem-solving by asking yourself a series of rational questions: "Is it true that I am worthless because people treat me that way? Can I accept myself and my human value even when others don't? Do I have to be thought of by others as perfect in order to live my life happily?" This process of thinking will deescalate your fight or flight response. "No, I don't need these behaviors from others to be content with myself. I would like people to behave differently, but sometimes they don't and I can certainly stand it."

EI takes a *bio-psycho-social perspective* on mental health awareness. Treating the whole person is expected to result in emotional wellness. Heightened attentiveness to one's biological response to thoughts will provide an individual with valuable information for emotional problem solving.

****

The theory of emotional intelligence we will be using might be described as *an acquired skill or ability for actively resolving emotional problems using a bio-psycho-social frame of reference*. Solving an emotional problem does not mean that the solution can only be one that brings you *happiness*. We are not trying to achieve happiness in the face of adversity. To do so would be an irresponsible and unachievable goal. If you make yourself angry, however, you can make yourself incrementally *less angry*. You might even make yourself content while in the midst of misfortune. *Positive incremental change* indicates success when improving EI.

In fact, the solutions you find while improving your EI might be, at times, simply *incremental*. You might, for instance, express anger x 10 when you encounter harsh conditions. But, using the skills found in this book, you may decrease your anger response to anger x 2.

Incremental change!

Celebrate it when it happens.

Improved emotional intelligence is not a search for an all or nothing emotional fix. In fact, there may be times when you maintain your anger without a single bit of change. Don't worry; if you wait long enough, time will take care of nearly all of your emotional issues. But if you can learn to *forgive yourself* for making yourself angry, while you wait for your anger to subside, you have been successful at improving your EI. Learning to forgive oneself for behaving foolishly is actually a significant sign of improved EI.

EI does not suggest that you will ever be happy when you are facing adversity, emotional challenge, bereavement, hardship or harsh conditions. It is very unlikely that you will ever use the skills found herein to move your emotions from anger to happiness. You can, however, achieve ***contentment*** where you would normally settle on ***discontent***.

Shit happens in life and I can still be happy when shit happens.

Prepare for the inevitability of incremental change.

****

Along with each old and new theory of EI, there seems to be a rather meandering use of new and old words and phrases – leading to more and more clarification – each clarification leading to endlessly more detail. So, EI teaching often includes a brave attempt at trying to stay clear and concrete in what may seem at times extraordinarily confusing. Without precision in your guide's choice of words and phrases, you, the learner, will likely be lost, or even (forbid) uninterested – defeating both of your purposes.

I am reminded of a learner who came to me wholly intent on becoming an expert in emotional intelligence.

She gave herself a six-week deadline.

While I sat explaining the model, one fraught with complex sociological terms and biopsychosocial jargon, I noticed she was fighting off sleep. The whites of her eyes replaced her irises, right in the middle of my enthusiastic explanation of all things – the limbic system!

Can you imagine?

And this was a willing and well-intentioned learner!

The empirical evidence to support my theory of EI may be (for me) irrefutable. I learned from my learner that day, however, that the value of my message may lie in how it is articulated – and how often I break for laughter.

I now know that maneuvering through the world of feelings, and trying to convey to others the often-confusing (and conflicting) philosophies related to emotion, is best achieved using as little lingo as possible. What lingo I do use, I like to make less complicated – more pedestrian; more consumable by the average consumer. I am also now very careful not to take myself so seriously and to add a bit of humor to what I am teaching. (Nothing is funnier, and more beneficial, than when we can laugh at ourselves.) After all, EI education is not about how crafty and illusive your guide can be while trying to help you improve your EI.

Neither is it intended to be a comedy show.

It's a balance.

An EI guide must pledge to pay more attention to the preciseness of h/er words and avoid the breadth and width of h/er boundless enthusiasm to explain everything. Improving one's EI is hard enough without making it deliberately humorless and more difficult.

****

If you truly intend to build a new foundation for your emotional intelligence, that project may become your ***enduring*** challenge. Some may even say *herculean*. Once you start the process of improvement, you may have to continue improving for the remainder of your lifetime – just to maintain your initial gains.

It won't take a lot of time to fall right back into your old way of emotional problem solving.

You cannot dabble in the improvement of EI.

You have to be committed.

I frequently tell my learners that behavior change (particularly with regard to emotion and its corresponding expression) is sometimes harder to achieve than moving an office building (or any building for that matter) two inches to the left. Your effort to improve your emotional intelligence may seem like that at times. Regaining and maintaining mental health and *emotional independence* are a tough slog! If you're committed to achieving a more *balanced* emotional state, you can do it.

You just have to be committed to hard slogging.

Personally, I have been endeavoring daily since 1992 to achieve my own improved EI. Previous to 1992, when **A** happened I *thought* **B** and I *felt* **C** without breaking a sweat.

I didn't give it a ***second thought***.

One thing I know for sure; undoing years of *unintelligent emotional development* will likely take me the rest of my life. Discovering that there are other emotional options – a broader array of letters from which to choose – and then committing to achieving a more ***manageable emotion*** took a lot of work.

For me, emotional evolution, even now, takes a bit of slogging.

We will never be happy that things don't go our way. Additionally, we will never be happy when we are treated ***disrespectfully, impolitely, boorishly*** or in some recognizably *foul*

manner. But when you learn how to ***think twice***, change is almost immediately achieved. You can be *less* angry and more forgiving.

If you **WANT** to!

That is always a possibility.

****

As opposed to trying to make you ***emotionless***, we will be addressing those emotions you would rather live without or that you would like to at least make ***incrementally less self-defeating***. Your efforts to improve your EI will be directed at those emotions that you find are ***unmanageable***.

Manageable anger.

Less depression.

A smaller amount of guilt.

The key word is ***unmanageable***. You are not being instructed on how to become unaffected; only how to manage those emotions that you express that have an impact on your expression of happiness. For example, *less anger* is better than ***more anger***. ***Sadness*** is much more manageable than ***depression***. ***Forgiveness*** is much more manageable than ***blame*** and ***guilt***.

The most we can ever hope for when encountering misfortune is ***contentment*** (which is a variation of happiness). We can be content that we have a higher standard for our own behavior. We can also be *sad* that people exercise their perfect right to act foolishly. *Forgiveness* and *sadness* are often far more manageable than *anger* and *rage*. Forgiveness and sadness are, as well, easily integrated into a more ***diverse definition of happiness***. Anger, for example, is often a product of your ***first thought***. Your evolved emotion, ***contentment***, ***sadness*** and *forgiveness*, your manageable emotions, will be a product of your *second thought*.

Enduring, long-lasting and permanent happiness may not even be a prospect of wo/mankind. If it isn't one thing, it's another. If you win the lottery, you will be worried that time passes too quickly for you to spend all your money, or maybe people are taking advantage of you or maybe you have lost your drive to succeed at the things you used to dream about. With that in mind, it may be best to view life as an inevitable series of ups and downs – never so good it couldn't be unpleasant and never so bad that it couldn't be better. Your personal definition of happiness may take these factors into consideration. There are three rules to enduring happiness. Unfortunately no one really knows what they are.

****

In times of misfortune, your *first thought*, your initial self-talk, is likely what brings you to experience **unmanageable emotions**. Left to itself, your first thought starts its cycle inside your head. Your first thought takes on momentum, instigating a neurological and hormonal cycle. Your anger can increase, the longer this cycle continues, resulting in chronic stress and emotional fatigue. Your *second thought*, however, will be more likely to lead you to a more rapid recovery from harmful, unmanageable emotions.

Managing a higher level of EI commands the more daunting challenge of *thinking twice* – once for the way you *used to think* and another for how you will *learn to think*. We will learn to hear our self-talk, understand it from a more informed perspective and evolve it to produce a more manageable emotional response.

It can be done!

I do it all day.

Ultimately, with practice and time, you will learn to live a more emotionally-managed, emotionally intelligent life.

****

It will be important to mention, before we proceed, how we will measure your EI improvement. Simply, your success and failure at improving EI will be judged by a *self-perceived measure*. There really is not emotional intelligence quotient. Emotional intelligence is an intuitive measure. Fundamentally, only you will know if your emotional intelligence is improving. Only you will be capable of deciding on your level of emotional effectiveness and increased endurance. There are no standardized tests that will provide you with a more valuable measurement of how *you* identify, assess and make your emotions more manageable for you. If you don't like your level of EI, you can improve it! It would be antithetical to rely on others to judge how well you are progressing. Remember, most people are nuts and can't be trusted to give you a fair, unbiased evaluation of your EI.

Nothing can better bring you peace than yourself.

"If you want to survive in a crazy world, you have to be crazier than everyone else."

Two – *It*

The title of this book implies that you can improve your emotional intelligence simply by reading it. We shall endeavor here forth to achieve that objective. I promise you in advance, however, that it will take a great deal more than that single effort.

I should also make it clear that improved emotional intelligence is not a process of becoming **emotionless.** You cannot hope to achieve **emotional numbness** when facing inconvenience, discomfort or misfortune. Neither is it reasonable to think that you will ever be happy when shit happens.

On the contrary.

A goal to live emotionally isolated and psychologically guarded is widely believed to be counter-productive to improved emotional intelligence (EI) – resulting, instead, in antisocial behavior – an outcome that is **not** intended to be achieved by reading this book.

It is a natural phenomenon for humans to **congregate,** to **cooperate** (and to force cooperation, when necessary) and to **copulate** (in one form or another). Successful social assimilation might be measured by how much *give-and-take* an individual possesses when expressing these essential behaviors.

Fundamentally, it is *not* considered optimal human behavior to live free of human contact or conflict. Nature builds into each of us the capacity to *cooperate, congregate* and *copulate* as a means of helping us survive as a species. Conflict often arises when we attempt to express any of these three essential behaviors in some manner contrary to the expected standard. Conflict is an instrument of *teaching* and *learning* and is vital to our development as humans. The challenge we face as a species, however, is in teaching everyone *the same rules* of interpersonal engagement we learned from our own parents, social contacts, communities and unique experiences.

That is not, at this very moment, possible.

So we will endeavor to work within that reality.

In the absence of some *perfect agreement* that details what single culture, which particular value system, distinct religion, sports team, type of food, unique point of view and behavior is appropriate for everyone, people will continue to engage in conflict. Some will learn from the experience and some will continue to act as if their unique and distinctive upbringing, their emotional education was unfaultable and that everything would be ever-so-much better *if only everyone else would just change the way they behave.*

The randomness and imprecision of how people express emotion is one of the more compelling reasons for improving one's emotional intelligence (EI). If you want to survive in a crazy world, you have to be crazier than everyone else. In other words, we must learn to live together knowing full well that we often share significantly different realities. Your emotional survival will depend on how well you adjust to that fact.

****

One of the more common misconceptions, irrespective of where they are acquired, is the idea that *your emotions are a result of how others treat you*.

"You *made* me angry!"

"She *makes* me miserable."

"*They irritate the piss out of me.*"

Let's just cut to the chase.

Your improved EI will depend on debunking the notion that *people make you feel*. These *very magical* phrases are like a virus infecting every last one of your brain cells. These phrases are so often heard and spoken, from the time you get up in the morning to the time you return to your bed, you may not even be prepared to even comprehend the magnitude of *silliness* you are accommodating.

"You *make me feel* like shit!"

Essentially, by accommodating this silly statement (by accepting that your emotions come from sources outside your control), you've committed to feeling like shit until you find someone who will *make you feel unlike shit*. In order to feel unlike shit, people must treat you kindly, respectfully, forgivingly, impartially, humanely and gently **AT ALL TIMES.** If they don't, you are likely, again, to turn into a pile of shit.

That manner of thinking is pure, unadulterated . . . shit!

When you *externalize the source of your emotions*, when you think your emotions come from how others treat you, you are likely not making improvement to your EI. Besides, if you place the blame for your ***shittiness*** on other people (including strangers), you are likely to feel shitty a lot of the time.

YOU make **YOURSELF** feel!

You make yourself feel by what you tell yourself about how people behave, how things turn out or how much you cannot stand the results you are facing.

"You made me feel like shit!"

"Really? How did I do that?"

"You criticized my hot pants at church!"

"How is that a problem for you?"

"You shouldn't criticize me. I'm your husband!"

"How is it a problem that your wife criticizes you?"

"People laughed at me and thought I was a clown."

"Are you a clown?"

"No."

"OK, you lost me. How did I make you feel like shit?"

****

As you progress with your EI improvement (and you begin to take responsibility for your own emotions) you may feel compelled to tell people that ***they*** (not you) are solely responsible for their own emotions. "I don't make you feel like shit. You do that to yourself. You tell yourself something about how I am behaving and ***you make yourself feel*** like shit. Change what you tell yourself about what I am doing, maybe forgive me or feel sorry for me, and you are likely to feel better almost immediately."

As you grow more comfortable with this idea that ***you make yourself feel***, you might want to explain to people that you had very little to do with creating their shitty emotions.

You might add, "Furthermore, you set off a *fight-flight-or-freeze* impulse in your brain. It was automatic, in fact. You sent all sorts of neurochemicals and hormones into your bloodstream and started this sort of domino effect. It's like your pituitary gland sent substances to your adrenal glands, into your heart and other major organs. It is really amazing! It would be best if you just breathed deeply and thought about what you are telling yourself about my behavior. That way you can get in touch with your thoughts and the feelings **YOU** are making, thoughts that make you feel like shit."

Or, you may want to hold off for a while.

This compulsion you will develop to express the true source of your emotions (and the true source of all emotion) will do little to help you satisfy your innate drive to *congregate, cooperate* or *copulate* with others.

People will stop talking to you.

****

It may seem strange to you at this point in your reading to learn that people don't make you feel – *that you make yourself feel*. I tell you early, and I give you fair warning, because I want you to get used to hearing it.

You will hear it a lot.

The complete premise of this book is built on that foundation.

People who are not actively involved in the process of improving their own EI will **NOT** want to hear anything about how they make themselves feel. Most people are quite content to believe that you and others are complicit in making them angry, depressed enraged, infuriated and happy. Removing yourself from that equation will not be well-tolerated.

People simply will not understand.

"You made me angry!"

"Goodness, how did I do that?"

"You handed me this instead of that."

"I think *you made yourself angry*."

"No, I don't *think* so. If you just behave the way I think you should, none of this would have happened in the first place."

"I am not comfortable having that much control over your emotions."

****

Before we go too far, I also want to discourage you from thinking this book has any connection to the *clichés* and *catch-phrases* you already use to manage your emotions. It may be best to just pretend you have no emotional coping skills at all and that you are here to learn from scratch. It's much like when I try to help my brother over the telephone with his computer problems. "Don't do anything until I tell you what to do. That way I know where we are in the process." Inevitably, my brother does what he likes, clicking here and there until I have no idea what is going on. "OK," I say, "Close everything and let's start all over. Let's pretend you have no idea what you're doing. Don't anticipate me! Let's begin from step one again."

Besides, my theory of EI isn't old enough to have developed a cliché or a catch-phrase. Suffice it to say, this book will **NOT** push you to solve your emotional problems by doing anything you already know – unless you've read *Go Suck a Lemon*. I will not be asking you to tell yourself **IT** doesn't bother you; that you should ignore **IT** or that you should close your eyes to **IT**. We will, instead, learn to identify **IT**, open our eyes wider to **IT** and make better sense of **IT**. Likewise, you will not be encouraged to sum up your emotional problems simply by saying, "**IT**'s OK." In fact, **IT** will never be **OK** that you are treated badly or rudely or offensively. It's foolishness to think otherwise. Pretending that **IT** is **OK** in the face of misfortune will do nothing to improve your EI. Thinking that **IT** is *awful, horrible* and *that you cannot stand it,* however, is taking **IT** a bit too far.

We will find a contented medium.

"I'm not OK with your behavior, because it isn't something I would allow myself to do. But I can live contentedly, regardless of your choices."

****

As our culture continues to accept the phrases, "He makes me so mad," and "They piss me off," as balanced, sane and reasonable explanations for the source of their emotions, we will be forever a culture of nuts. These phrases, although quite common, are nothing more than products of magical thinking. You will be moving exponentially forward if you take a moment to examine the veracity of these statements and conclude that continuing to speak this way leaves little potential for improvement in emotional intelligence (EI). The fact is – no experience, circumstance or event has intrinsic meaning; *events unto themselves are meaningless until we apply meaning to them*.

The individual application of meaning is the impetus for emotion.

Meaning, however, abounds, varying to some degree from one person to another. Meaning can differ slightly or it can diverge to such a degree that getting the basic facts of an event can become an exercise in utter bewilderment. We are likely to apply as many meanings to the same situation, circumstance or event as there are people experiencing it.

In my quest to encourage the concept of taking personal responsibility for one's own emotions, my learner often makes a quick adjustment in semantics, replacing the phrase, "It made me feel," with the more rational declaration, "I made myself feel." That progress in sanity, however grand, is often impeded when the learner begins to describe h/er emotional upsettedness using the phrase, "I let it make me feel;" as if letting something make h/er feel is a rational replacement for describing the source of one's emotional problems.

The phrase "I let it make me feel," implies a shared responsibility for one's emotions.

That simple concession in responsibility **will not do**.

Improvement in EI requires ***taking full responsibility*** for one's emotions. If EI improvement is your goal, responsibility for your emotions cannot be shared with anyone or anything.

Ever.

When working with learners, I am often left with either ignoring this variation in semantics, or pointing out the illogical thinking. Of course I choose the latter and I am almost always faced with a learner who is baffled.

"I thought I was making progress."

"Well, you are. There is still more to know."

It is one thing to explain to the learner, "You cannot let something make you feel if it doesn't and never has had the ability to do that in the first place." It is quite another to explain this notion in terms that are not so meandering and convoluted that I lose the learner's ambition to improve at all.

I will make my best effort.

Believing that you can *allow* or *let* people make you feel, on its surface, is an hysterical notion and is wholly batty. In order to accept this idea, one must first agree that people, in fact, possess super powers that can, if allowed to do so, subdue you and make you feel emotion. Leaving you with no other option than to submit to that magical power or thwart its influence over your emotions. (Something like holding up a shield to the thunderbolt of energy that intends to bring you down, emotionally.) People do not have magical authority over how you feel and, so, cannot be *allowed* or *let* to influence your emotions – whether you want them to or not.

Only you can do that.

You have always made yourself feel.

There really are no other excuses for it.

Your feelings, your emotions are NOT a shared responsibility.

In my experiences, it seems that people are somewhat prone to make strides in their EI, after being introduced to the concept that their emotions come from their thoughts about situations, events and circumstances. It's not a hard sell, really. "You make yourself feel by the way you think," followed by some explanation of the workings of the brain, and the wonders of improved EI are set in motion.

I do not often run into much push back on that account.

Of course, as you may have figured out already, actually doing something with that knowledge is an altogether separate issue. This phenomenon of *forbearing to do without actually doing* can be described as *intellectual insight* without corresponding behavioral change. Learners easily understand the biopsychsocial connection between their thinking and emotion, but they are often reluctant to do anything more than appreciate that concept.

Emotion is a product of biology, psychology and social learning. Social learning often includes perception, interpretation and the application of meaning. These three components are unique to each individual and share little connection to external phenomena. Essentially, shit happens and you apply meaning to it. The more meaning you apply to shit the stronger your emotional connection to shit will be.

The belief that you are letting or not letting something bother you is an alternative, more subtle, way of externalizing the source of your emotion. It's pretty much like saying, "I make myself feel," only you are holding on to the idea that something outside of you still influences your feelings. The phrase is something of a hold out, an individual's way of not fully accepting h/er responsibility for h/er emotions without at least attributing some part of the emotional source to something external.

To truly make improvement in EI, you will have to take FULL responsibility for your emotions. You cannot imply or even allude to the idea that your emotions come from anything other than yourself. People don't make you feel and you don't let or not let things, circumstances, events or happenings make you feel.

You always make yourself feel, regardless of the stimulus.

Emotion is always a result of your own perception, interpretation and the meaning you apply to stimuli. So, as you grow in your pursuit of EI, the most beneficial step you can take is assuming responsibility for every emotion you feel – while not falling for the idea that something outside yourself is magically making, producing or stimulating that emotion.

If you know someone who can truly make others feel emotion, sign h/er to a contract and join the circus together.

****

As far as I know, people do not have magical powers, wands, spells or special elixirs to *make* others feel emotion. (I am personally overjoyed that people don't have the power to *actually make me feel* like shit.) The only power that people do have to make us feel is that we *think* they can.

It's much like being hypnotized.

If you want to believe you are a chicken, it is very possible that you will behave like a chicken. (Whether you actually feel like a chicken, or feel like a human who is acting like a chicken, is yet another topic for another book.) Besides, if people truly did have the power to *make* us feel, they could just as easily *make* us *un-feel*. This very *"magical making"* doesn't seem to work as well going in the opposite direction.

This idea that others make us feel is all quite foolish, when you think about it.

Besides, who would want to grant that kind of power to others?

Even if it were possible that people could make you feel, wouldn't you be trying to find a way to prevent it, rather than accommodate it day after day?

The idea that *people make you feel* is such a phenomenon, a national crisis in fact, it seems there would be hundreds if not thousands of inventions to **STOP IT**! Surely someone would have invented an emotional force field by now. The *Home Shopping*

Network would be inundated with orders for the *new* and *improved* **Emotional Force Field** by *Ronco* in twelve designer colors, styles and wash-and-wear fabrics. We could all wear one – maybe a helmet, a wristband, a bodysuit or antennae – and whenever someone tried to *make* us feel we would repel that bad magic.

Pure nuts!

There is one device that I know of that even comes very close to repelling people and their magical ability make us feel.

Ear plugs.

****

In addition to believing that others *make* you feel, you make things even worse by telling yourself that your happiness depends on how others choose to treat you. Essentially, "I cannot live my life happily until you change your behavior. I need you to behave differently and I will be angry until you change to suit me."

And you wonder why you see so many angry people walking around? Everyone is waiting for everyone else to change their behavior so they can resume their happy lives.

STOP WAITING!

Change *your own* behavior by learning to *think differently*. People will behave any way they choose, regardless of how you feel about it – unless you have something they want. Then they will change for just as long as it takes to get it.

Be proactive with yourself.

Take advantage of your brain's ability to be *flexible* with the information you feed it.

You can stand it!

If the source of your happiness comes from how well people treat you, you are likely to be unhappy a lot of the time. At least, of course, until they allow you to feel happy, which will last just as long as it takes for them to change their mind. At minimum, for now, if you don't like how people behave, at least stop telling yourself you *can't stand it*.

The more you believe you can stand something the more you will likely stand it. As a matter of fact, you could very well stand it if you were held down and had pins stuck in your eyeballs all day. You can get used to about anything if it happens to you long enough.

If you have ever been in a room with a child who just got a new trumpet, you may think you've met the threshold of your *frustration tolerance*. You haven't. Anyway, it is far more tolerable to stand that people act foolishly than it would be to be held down and have pins stuck in your eyeballs.

****

One of the unfortunate consequences of improving your EI is that, as you do truly come to **BELIEVE** that you and only you make yourself feel, people will continue to blame you for how *they* are feeling. You will have to fain responsibility, in order to get along – *cooperate, congregate* and *copulate*. "I'm sorry I *made* you *angry, sad, depressed* and *unhappy*. I accept full responsibility for that. Can I make you happy again?"

If people can blame others for their feelings, they don't have to take responsibility for how they are making themselves feel. People don't like to accept responsibility for their own emotions. If you are willing to be responsible for everyone's emotions, however, people will almost always like you more – especially if you apologize, accept culpability and bend and sway every time someone needs to assign a source of their emotional state to someone else.

"YOU made me angry!"

"Goodness, really? I had no idea."

"I can't stand it when people do what you just did."

"What can I do to make you happy?"

"You can stop doing that!"

"Are there any other options?"

"No."

"But if I do that I will be unhappy."

"That's your problem."

****

Our culture heavily endorses the idea that other people make them feel. You will have to work against that idea, while also living peacefully with the multitudes of people who seek just the opposite effect. You should know early, however, that no matter how much you improve your EI, nutty people will likely maintain control over nearly everything.

Be nice to them.

They own most of the surface of the planet; they are often the objects of our affection, and they are decidedly in control of much of the world's food supply. Your physical survival depends on cooperating with nutty, magical people.

****

Improving your emotional intelligence is **NOT** a goal you can set and achieve once-and-for-all.

Quite the opposite.

As long as you are living and *conscious* you will have an emotional life. A **commitment** to achieving better emotional results will likely be a goal you will have to pledge to pursue for the rest of your time among others. If you take this material seriously, you will ***always*** be challenged to ***think more than once*** when you encounter ***adversity***, when people who ***behave poorly*** or when you find a gray hair – in your soup. Your desire to strive to maintain a life that includes better EI will be up to you.

I am only a *guide*.

****

I am forever reminded of how much emphasis for achievement in EI therapy is placed on the EI guide and so little on the learner.

"The EI guide didn't do anything. *It* didn't work."

"Yeah, he sucks. It didn't do a thing for me, either."

"I'm done with it."

"I need a pill."

"Me, too, my nerves are a mess."

"What do you have?"

NEWS! FLASH!

EI theory isn't supposed to work!

You're supposed to work.

As a matter of fact, there is no evidence that therapy of any kind, as an agent of change in mental health is any better than no therapy at all. The therapist, from my limited estimation, is more likely to simply keep you company while your emotional problems run their course. Therapy may even be less effective than simple *time*. The more time that passes, the less emotionally upset an individual can expect to become.

That *depression* you had after the divorce – **GONE**! with time.

That *anxiety* you had after moving – **GONE**! with time.

That *anger* you had after being fired – **GONE**! with time.

So why are we talking at all about this issue – this EI theory? If therapy doesn't work, and I can just wait for enough time to pass, why am I reading this book at all?

Good question (if I say so myself).

In contrast to the kind of therapy you're used to seeing or hearing about on TV or reading about on your Kindle, enhancing your EI will result in your increased capacity to endure *future challenges* to your emotional balance. Improvement in your EI may result in you spending less time waiting for your problems to just go away. Besides, no sooner are they gone than they're back again, making improvement in EI even more essential. EI will help you become your own emotional problem-solver, strengthening your resolve for the next time shit happens. You will acquire skills for:

- ***Independence*** from judgments made by others, helping you rely more on your own judgment of yourself;
- Discouraging ***emotional conformity*** by encouraging ***emotional range***;
- Encouraging ***emotional self-determination***;
- Valuing ***self acceptance*** over the concept of self esteem; and,
- ***Solving*** your own emotional problems, resulting in better preparation for the next time shit happens.

****

Finally, there is no compelling support for the familiar paradigm of one therapist and one patient, or ten patients and two guards, thirty random people and one leader or any other formation of the therapeutic alliance that is any better than simply talking to yourself – ***using articulated thought***.

(We will learn to do that, too.)

Of course articulated thought without some direction may be a muddle. Knowing the right things to say to oneself, however, is the key; although, babbling to oneself may resemble, in a lot of ways, the kind of therapy that is available today from your local mental health center.

In today's world, it is best to keep as much of your mental health under your own control as possible; as opposed to turning it over to others as a *first option*.

You can learn to help yourself.

Your mental health is one of those coveted possessions best guarded against preventable damage.

Nothing can better bring you peace than yourself.

*"Of course using **articulated thought** without some direction may be a muddle. Knowing the right things to say to oneself, however, is the key."*

Three – *I'm wired!*

As fleeting as the thought may be, you do **think at least once** before responding to nearly any emotional stimuli. **Happiness, anger, joy, sadness** – each emotion is preceded by thought. It is a very rapid, almost unidentifiable thought; but a thought nonetheless.

Much of your work at improving your EI will be directed at distinguishing your emotions from your thinking and learning to capture that often-illusive ***first thought***. (Of course familiarity with your first thought is essential to building a second thought. It is unlikely you can think twice if you aren't aware that you think once.) Your second thought will be shaped into what you may later come to know as your ***evolved emotion***.

You might imagine from grade school the chart depicting developing wo/mankind, starting with the illustration of a small, hunched-over ape who progressively transforms into the upstanding creature we know h/er to be today. That illustration is essentially the progress your emotions will take, once you learn to capture your first thought and *evolve* it from a small, primitive ape-like creature into something more representative of civilized humanity.

Identifying your first thought and preparing it for evolution may be your biggest challenge right now. I often ask my learners to tell me what they told themselves – what their thoughts were, just before they made themselves angry. Inevitably I get a very confused look and then, "What did I tell myself? What do you mean? I didn't tell myself anything. Are you implying I hear voices in my head?"

"Yes, sort of; just listen to your thoughts. What are you telling yourself?"

"I'm not telling myself anything. I can't think. I'm too angry to think! If I'm telling myself anything, I'm telling myself I'd like to kick that guy in the neck."

"How have you determined you should kick him in the neck?"

"How? Well I can look at him and figure that out."

"How have you determined that?"

"Because he did that and said this and he shouldn't behave that way."

"How should he behave?"

"He should do things right."

"All the time?"

"Yes."

"So what are you telling yourself?"

Capturing your thoughts isn't really a very difficult process. We have a long-running, very familiar dialogue with ourselves every day that is easily recognizable. The problem may be that the question sounds so bizarre, *"What are you telling yourself?"* asked at a time when most people are confronted not with how they are making themselves feel, but how they believe *others are making them feel*.

Reconciling that struggle is essential to hearing what you are telling yourself.

It seems so much easier to ask, "What was the other person telling h/erself when *they were making you* angry?" To which the learner is always glad to tell me. "S/he was telling h/erself that s/he was better than me and that s/he was going to show me. She was, like, giving me the finger; but not really; but sort of."

"How did you know s/he was doing all that?"

"I could tell by h/er face."

"So what were you telling yourself about her face?"

"Like I said, I wasn't telling myself anything except I wanted to kick it."

****

To begin to address this very simple yet confusing issue, we might have a quick look at a concept known as locus of control (LC). Developed by Julian Rotter in the 1950s, the concept of LC was established to identify an individual's perceived source of control over h/er destiny, fortune and fate – and emotion.

There are believed to be two variations on this concept: *internal locus of control* (ILC) and *external locus of control* (ELC). If, for example, you take a test and you fail, do you attribute the cause of that outcome to a lack of studying (ILC)? Or that your teacher didn't like you (ELC)?

The notion of LC can easily be applied to the concept of emotional intelligence. LC is related to whom you attribute the cause of your *emotional behavior* – to yourself or others? Individuals with an ILC view their emotional state as a result of their own thinking and behaving – *something under their control*. People with an ELC view their emotions as being under the control of external factors, such as the way other people behave toward them.

- An ILC is like looking in a mirror and seeing yourself.
- An ELC is like looking in a mirror and seeing someone else.

LC may have a profound effect on overall psychological well-being. If people feel they have no control over their emotions (that the cause of how they feel comes from something external of them), they are less likely to seek or apply solutions to their emotional problems. The far-reaching effects of such maladaptive behaviors can have serious consequences in many areas of life.

It appears that expressing an ILC is more beneficial for improving emotional intelligence than expressing an ELC. A person must perceive that s/he has control over those things s/he is capable of influencing, particularly the source of h/er emotions, before s/he is likely to be successful at controlling h/er emotions.

The first step in developing ILC competence is to pay attention to what you tell yourself when you are experiencing emotion –

especially emotion that you believe to be *unmanageable*. Listen to your internal dialogue when you are facing hardship.

Hear that voice.

It will tell you everything you need to know.

That voice is your *first thought*, the one we must learn to capture. The first thought that will lead you to your second thought and to your recovery.

An efficient ILC usually needs to be matched by *competence, self-efficacy* and *opportunity* so that the person is able to successfully experience a sense of personal control and responsibility. Improved emotional intelligence emphasizes an ILC and provides a method for gaining *competence* and *value*. The *opportunity* to practice will be available to you every day.

****

Oddly, it is far more possible to discover what a person is telling h/erself when s/he is expressing happiness and joy. There is no surprise, no faltering, no hesitation when a person hears, "You're happy! What are you telling yourself right now?"

"I'm glad you asked! I am telling myself that I am going to get what I *always* wanted for Christmas and *that* is wonderful and I will finally be happy. I will now finally be able to do what I had hoped to do. Everything will be so perfect, so much easier for me. I'll be on Easy Street like I knew someday I would be. I'm going to be successful and everyone will love me!"

In my experience, people are forever so much more forthcoming with what they tell themselves when they are making themselves joyful. But asking people what they are telling themselves when they are making themselves **angry, depressed, livid** or **gnashing their teeth** is often so much more difficult.

It's a mystery that we will solve later.

For now, keep listening for your inner voice.

***

If you're under the age of one, it may be possible for you to respond to the world with more emotional *flexibility* than an adult. (Those of you who are under the age of one can stop reading now and run along. If you can write, please jot down your thoughts on EI and send them to me. I would be forever grateful to, once again, have the emotional resolve and flexibility of a one-year-old.) If you're over the age of one, dig in your heels. Your EI adventure is all very possible; it just gets progressively more difficult as you age.

A child's emotional possibilities are boundless – from **A** to **Z** and back again. An adult, on the other hand, often loses h/er emotional flexibility as s/he ages, running the broad spectrum, instead, from **A** to **C** and back again. Where children can choose from hundreds of options to express emotion, adults often confine themselves to only a few.

This happens, *I feel anger*.

This happens, *I feel depression*.

This happens, *I feel anxiety*.

This happens, *I feel joy*!

With very limited variation.

Choosing *irrationality* over *rationality* leaves us with the burden of overcoming a number of cognitive and structural (biological) **barriers** that children do not yet possess.

Children learn from adults the ***proper*** way to perceive any given circumstance and express emotion within a particular cultural model.

When is ***anger*** a fitting response?

When do I express ***glee***?

What do I do when I am ***jealous***?

Children often play out their roles with toys, experimenting with scripts, rehearsing roles and solidifying their future places in society. One lesson builds upon another until the child suddenly realizes that what separates h/er from being viewed as a mature, emoting adult is that adults don't rehearse anymore. Children come to view the transition to adulthood as a forfeiture of their toys for ***inflexibility*** and ***rigidity*** in thinking and behaving.

Toys, however, might be made more purposeful in the resolution of adult problems.

I suggest getting some Barbie dolls and GI Joes and playing out different resolutions to the same emotional issues. Try having Barbie ***forgive*** Joe for his careless behavior. Have Joe express ***sadness*** that Barbie is behaving ***foolishly***. Try out ***new scripts*** and ***roles*** before committing to them. Regaining a child's creativity when faced with solving emotional questions may be what we are all trying, once again, to regain.

****

The exchange of old ideas for new ones can be lost without continued vigilance. It is ***not atypical***, for example, to hear the phrase, "She ***made*** me so mad." This statement, of course, is heard in approximately 70 different languages, every day, from one end of the planet to the other. You may have even said it yourself more than once today.

"That driver pissed me off!"

"She is late and I can't stand it!"

We have cultivated the impulse to blame our emotions on things that are outside our control. *I am mad, and you did it. I am depressed and you did that too. I am going to kill you because you left me with no other choice. You are only alive because I don't want to go to jail!*

All of it NUTS!

The endless social reinforcement that favors **irrationality** – *You made me angry!* – over **rationality** – *I make myself angry because I told myself I NEED your cooperation in order to be happy in my life*, makes the sorting out of old and new thinking a challenge for most adults.

The fact is, people don't make you feel.

You ***think about*** how others are behaving and ***your thoughts*** make you feel. No situation, circumstance or state of affairs is meaningful until ***you bring meaning to it***. When you take responsibility for your thoughts you are taking the first step toward improved emotional responsibility. You are more likely to contribute to the resolution of your emotional upsettedness if you know what role you played in creating it ***and*** sustaining it. It would be foolish (if not nutty) to believe that you cannot be happy until others behave in ways that **SUIT** you and meet your imagined **NEEDS**.

Own your own emotional problems.

****

Children are more liable than adults to make better progress learning to manipulate their thinking and emotions. After all, children are *wired for social learning.* It's pretty much all they do from birth to adolescence, after which time they start to independently use the lessons they learned in a broader spectrum of society.

You are still wired this way.

You just need a strong reminder.

You learned a long time ago to *act your age* and leave behind anything about yourself that wasn't *age appropriate.* Your *flexible emotional resolve* was one of those cherished gifts you left behind. You replaced *resolve* with *inflexible beliefs*. We will have to find a way to overcome that.

In his *Guide to Rational Living*, Albert Ellis (my personal hero) describes the most damaging *beliefs* common to most people. I refer to these nine beliefs as:

Terms of Enragement

1. The belief that you **HAVE TO** be *loved* and *approved of* by all the *significant* people in your life. In the absence of cooperation, you can never be *truly* happy.
2. The belief that you **SHOULD** always be completely competent, productive and successful. If you're not, you are a failure and can never be truly happy.
3. The belief that people **OUGHT** to never act obnoxiously or unfairly toward you or toward people you care about. If that happens, you can never be truly happy.
4. The belief that people who act foolishly, make poor choices or behave irresponsibly **SHOULD** be damned.

5. The belief that you **HAVE TO** view things you don't like as awful, terrible, horrible and catastrophic.
6. The belief that you **MUST** be miserable and unhappy when you have pressures and difficult experiences and that you **CANNOT** be happy in your life until you have no difficulties.
7. The belief that you have **VERY LITTLE CONTROL** over your disturbed feelings and you cannot be happy until you do.
8. The belief that the past will always influence and will forever determine your feelings and behavior in the present and you cannot be happy because of that.
9. The belief that people and things absolutely **MUST** be better than they are and you cannot be happy until they are.

These nine beliefs represent what we teach children and re-teach ourselves about individual emotional potential every day. These beliefs often become the framework from which children build an understanding of their social worlds. Children have greater potential to utilize their brain's plasticity (ability to *think differently*) and their innate trait for *emotional flexibility*. In fact, we all have the potential for emotional flexibility, at any age. We just don't use it much after we put away our toys. We might better express these nine absolute beliefs as:

Terms of Engagement

1. The belief that you can experience disapproval and dissatisfaction from others without concluding that criticism is proof of your worthlessness as a human being.

2. The belief that you can make mistakes, learn, take chances, express and change your opinion, and fail without concluding that you are a complete failure.
3. The belief that people do not have to behave perfectly or according to your standards in order for you to be happy living a world with them.
4. The belief that people who act foolishly, make poor choices or behave irresponsibly can be excused, pardoned and forgiven.
5. The belief that experiencing things you don't like are *temporary inconveniences*. If you increase your frustration tolerance for things you don't like, you will be more comfortable the next time the same or similar shit happens.
6. The belief that your life will include experiences that are unpleasant and that you will never be free of all difficulties.
7. The belief that you and only you control how you think and therefore how you feel.
8. The belief that your past has as much influence over your present as you think it does.
9. The belief that people and things are the way they are and if you're in a better frame of mind, people will be more likely to hear you and you may be in a better position to strengthen your relationships with others.

****

Imagine that you pick up your child at the daycare and you arrive home only to find your house has burned to the ground.

Imagine your response.

On average, an adult will respond *hysterically*.

"What will I do now? I have to call someone! My pictures! My mother's quilt! My cat! My penny jar! I'm ruined! Where is my mailbox?"

Whereas a child may look at the wonder of the smoldering embers and ask, "Can I get a new Nintendo?"

"Can we make a tent out of blankets and live in it?"

"Can we live with Joey?"

"Should we call Daddy?"

"You don't have to cry. We can live in the car."

As the caregiver and child go further into the process of resolving the tragedy, the child will learn from the adult how to be less flexible with h/er emotional potential and respond to future unfortunate events the way s/he has been taught. This example of ***experiential emotional memory*** can be applied to nearly any event in a child's life. Fundamentally, children develop an emotional memory based on how their caregivers teach them to behave and emote.

Children, to a certain age, haven't yet trained themselves to emote in any strict, inflexible manner. They depend on adults to teach them. If their caregivers are inflexible in their emotional instruction, their children will be, as well. If the caregiver is more liberal, permissive or *laissez-faire*, the child will learn from that unique experience. (This is not an implied value judgment of how to raise children. This is an illustration of how children develop their ***emotional memory***.)

We are the adults our parents raised us to be.

We each carry an emotional memory that may not work well for us all the time. Children might be taught, for example, to fight when their friends criticize them. Children will grow up to express the same reaction to criticism by teachers, a loved one or a boss. Children can, as well, be taught to forgive people who act foolishly. And they will likely respond differently to criticism in adulthood, if we teach them a new way to do that. In fact, children can be taught any number of responses to adversity. Children can learn to ***think once*** and be quite successful for the remainder of their lives, if they are trained early and properly.

They frequently are not.

Case in point: You and I were once children; yet we are searching for a way to re-form our brains and promote better emotional intelligence. Sadly, some of our emotional education left to us by our parents and other teachers was not so life-enhancing.

I recently had an encounter with a parent who asked me my opinion on why people don't know how to resolve their differences. "What has gone wrong?" the mother asked. "People don't know how to talk to each other anymore. Even parents don't talk with each other about their child's behaviors anymore. We are such a grumpy bunch."

"It may have something to do with how we teach children to resolve their problems. We used to play outside, interact with other children and adults and resolve our problems in the community. Parents talked to parents. Children talked to each other. They learned to compromise and get along. Now, children stay home all day, play video games, chat on the computer and watch TV. And when they argue with family members, when they disagree or fight, we separate them – send them in different directions."

"Yeah, they need to ***cool off***."

"Then what?"

"They eventually play together again."

"What did they learn about resolving disagreements?"

"To separate? Not talk to each other?"

"Sure, and not learn to negotiate, collaborate or settle their dispute."

"I think I break them up for my own sanity more than their opportunity to learn."

"I think that may be true."

If I were bold enough, I would say that we have to surrender many of our rigid, inflexible beliefs about social behavior and go back to the beginning, to being a one-year-old – before we were infected with the nutty beliefs we have about ourselves and other people.

Before we gave up our toys and, in this case, our opportunities to learn from experience.

We may simply have to learn to think and behave all over again.

To **think twice**.

This time with *flexibility*!

****

Your belief in right and wrong, good and bad, best and better and your ability to distinguish one concept from the other is likely a very honorable system of judgment. Your beliefs illustrate for you what might be described as ideal behavior. Like you, however, people don't always behave ideally. That does not mean you should compromise your belief that people have a great deal of potential to behave more effectively. It does mean that you can make better choices in how you encounter weakness in others. Simply because people don't behave ideally does not mean they are bad or hopelessly flawed. It simply means that people are not always willing to cooperate with you and your estimation of how they should behave.

Noxious behavior unto itself does not render people irredeemable.

Hold on to your honorable beliefs about ideal behavior. Do your best to express your honorable beliefs in your own behavior. Remember, however, people don't always live by your expectations. In fact, you, yourself, don't always live up to the expectations you have of others.

We all fail on some level.

Everyone has a perfect right to behave foolishly. And they often exercise that perfect right. No one HAS TO treat you respectfully, honestly, favorably or kindly. If they do, it is because they chose to; NOT that you chose their behavior for them. And you can still be happy living in a world where this reality can be accommodated.

****

Most people are addicted to a ***certain kind*** of happiness.

"When everything is going this way, I am truly happy."

"What do you feel when things aren't going your way?"

"I guess I feel shitty."

"Can you change your definition of happiness?"

"I'm not sure."

"So it's either all happiness or nothing?"

"I guess."

Resolving that ***happiness*** can only be defined as pure, uninterrupted bliss may be your emotional downfall. Happiness, in order to be experienced more often, ***must include truths*** from the real world to be fully functional. You don't have to win the lottery, be on Easy Street, free of stress and anxiety, liked by everyone you meet or be young and beautiful to be happy. It is likely that if you had all of these things and more, you would still experience problems. If not for no other reason than you might be anxious, fearful and nervous about losing it all.

You do not NEED people to be considerate, empathetic, thoughtful, intelligent, selfless or brave for you to be happy. You do not NEED to pay all your bills, buy your dream car, have another baby or live in a mansion to be happy. Neither do you NEED to be thinner, weightier, more attractive, less or more hairy or have a college degree. In fact, if you're not enough without these things you will not be enough if you get them.

Things don't *make* you happy.

You make yourself happy or unhappy by what you tell yourself about things.

You really don't NEED anything. If you tell yourself you NEED something you will make yourself anxious and unhappy when you don't have it. If you tell yourself you WANT something, when you don't have it, you can live contentedly in spite of not having it.

Needing something and *wanting* it may be the difference between happy and unhappy.

Change your definition.

People can just as well choose to be inconsiderate, uncaring, thoughtless, foolish, selfish and cowardly and you can be content, in spite of it. And you can adjust and live contentedly in a world where you can expect that people will do just that.

Seeking ***unalterable definition of happiness*** will likely lead to occasional periods of happiness. Seeking happiness using a more logical, rational definition of how you will achieve happiness in a world that is **NOT** likely to bring you what you **NEED** all the time is likely to result in more and longer periods of contentment.

Considering that people behave according to their own standards, you might consider refashioning your definition of happiness to include that particular factor. You might also consider a definition of happiness that includes sadness, forgiveness, tolerance and patience. You can call it ***hap-i-licious***!

"How are you?"

"I'm ***hap-i-licious***."

"What does that mean?"

"It means I don't have to live in a ***perfect*** world to be happy. Everything doesn't have to be going my way for me to be happy - to be content. In fact, it is a pretty rare occasion when everything is going my way. I can tolerate people who behave badly. I can feel sad for people who make poor choices. I can forgive people who exercise their perfect right to behave fatally human."

"I want to be ***hap-i-licious***."

"You can. It takes time and effort, though."

****

One thing is for sure; your ***terms of engagement*** with others are **NOT** *laws, edicts* or *regulations* (except in your own head). If they were, we would all be in prison. Your flouted expectations become your terms of ***enragement***. If you want to make your thinking and emotions more flexible, begin by modifying your ***thinking***. Modify your ***thinking*** to include emotional possibility and flexibility. This evolution in your emotional behavior can be achieved by changing your viewpoint. You might start with viewing people who choose to act poorly in much the same way you would view the limitations of a **handicapped person**.

> An **emotionally handicapped** person.

You are likely to be more patient, considerate, helpful and unwearied of people who are viewed as emotionally handicapped. You can view people who choose to act noxiously toward you as people who are more in need of tolerance, endurance and lasting compassion, rather than anger, rage or anxiety.

> **Renegotiate your terms of enragement.**

I am not suggesting that you *celebrate* the weaknesses of others and congratulate them for showing you their failings (although you could). I am asking you, however, to recognize that those weaknesses exist in everyone, including yourself, in contrast to your expectations. We are all emotionally handicapped to some extent – especially when we leave the environment where we learned our emotional behavior and show up where no one understands anything we are doing or saying. Knowing that fact in advance will make encountering weakness in others (and yourself) more manageable.

****

People often behave contrary to your wishes. Their behavior, regardless, is *not* **NECESSARY** for your continued happiness.

If you are appreciative of this message, you may have had to stop and wonder – to *think twice* about it – once foolishly, *"What kind of shit is this?"* and the second in a more rational, reasoned and balanced way, resulting in added self-enhancing improvement, *"You're right! I don't* **need** *complete cooperation from others in order to find* *happiness in my life. I can live hap-i-liciously even when people don't cooperate with my demands on their behavior,"* or *"People don't have to behave the way I want them to behave. They can choose to behave foolishly. They have a perfect right to behave any way they want. I will never like it that people act so irresponsibly with one another, but I can still be hap-i-licious in my life even when they behave in ways that I don't like."*

***

I have found that maintaining improvement in EI, learning to **think twice**, requires effort, a higher level of *frustration tolerance* and a good dose of *self-determination*. The degree of effort you will use to improve your EI will depend on your level of commitment, where you have been and what you have experienced previous to reading this book. Greater *frustration tolerance* and *self-determination*, of course, are necessary to achieving any goal.

Nothing can better bring you peace than yourself.

*"Holding an **unalterable definition** of happiness will likely lead to occasional periods of happiness."*

Four – *I play the bitch role*

People are quite expert at expressing *self-defeating* emotional behaviors. It is this self-defeating behavior that contributes to trouncing our EI goals. People often prefer self-defeat over better, more self-enhancing thoughts and behaviors – EVEN when there is evidence showing that behaving differently would bring them better emotional results. You would be healthier, more resilient to disease, for example, if you experienced less anger; not to mention that if you express yourself peacefully, people are more likely to listen to your message. *That's all well and good*, you might think. *But it's easier to behave the way I always have.*

Of course!

Behaving the way you always have is less complicated. Your self-defeating behaviors, your *first thoughts*, are better rehearsed. You have a script for how to respond to nearly anything in your environment. It is effortless to play your familiar role (first thoughts) than to create an altogether new character (second thoughts).

"I have acted this way for my whole life."

"That's your excuse for being so angry?"

"Yes, it's the way I am."

"Maybe it's the role you play."

"Yeah, I play the *bitch* role a lot."

"You can change your role. Create a new character."

"Why should I? I would have to learn a whole new script."

"Change often requires the exertion of *effort*."

"I don't like effort."

Besides, people are not routinely interested in putting in effort to change their *own* behaviors. They want everyone else to change their behaviors to suit their own expectations. That sentiment is often heard in the phrase, "You **NEED** to change. You **NEED** to do what you're told. You **NEED** to be nicer to me." To which the only logical response is, "Who really **NEEDS** this?"

An even better example of this phenomenon can be found in therapy. People are forever coming to see me, telling me that they *cannot stand* their partner's behavior. They would be so much happier if their partner would just change.

"How is his behavior a problem for you?"

"I don't like it."

"Is that enough to make him change?"

"I guess not. I tell him but he never changes."

"What can *you* do about it?"

"I am not the problem. He is!"

"Can you have him come in to see me, instead?"

"He doesn't think he needs to change."

"How can I help you?"

People would rather deem themselves *right* and put their best effort into making everyone else behave.

"How dare you say that to me?"

"I will say anything I want to you!"

"You won't if I have anything to say about it!"

"You can't do anything about it."

"I can beat you."

"Yes, you can try that; but I will say what I want right afterward!"

"No you won't!"

"Yes I will!"

"No you won't!"

"Yes I will!"

"I'm exhausted."

"Me too."

"OK, let's fight and see how that works."

"Bring it."

Plainly, believing that *your* happiness depends on how others choose to behave toward you will endlessly interfere with your success in achieving that goal. People will do exactly as they please and will not often seek your approval before doing so.

"Excuse me. I am in a really shit-fried mood. I hate my job; I hate myself; I hate every choice I ever made in my life. I was wondering if you wouldn't mind if I treated you obnoxiously. I would really enjoy that."

"Oh, why not; I'm not busy right now. I have a hair appointment at three. Will it take long?"

"Not really. Just as long as it will take for me to ring up all this shit you're buying."

"OK, as long as it's quick. Thank you for asking, though. Otherwise I wouldn't have enjoyed the experience as much."

"No! Thank **YOU**! I wish more people would be as cooperative with my whims. Your hair really does need some help, by the way. You look like a boll weevil."

Likewise, people don't often **NEED** what you tell them they **NEED**. People will **NEED** exactly what they think they **NEED** and there is little anyone can do about it, short of violence, to change that. If you think that people **NEED** to treat you *respectfully, caringly, courteously, empathically* and with *focused interest* you may find that supposed **NEED** is merely an option they are **NOT** willing to accept from you. Except, of course, if you have something they want. Then they will behave exactly how you think they **NEED** to behave, in order to get it or to keep getting it.

The best method for improving your EI will be the application of leveled *reasoning* in your emotional decision-making.

"You *need* to be ashamed of yourself."

"Really? How have you determined that?"

"You are not acting right. You're acting foolishly."

"And I *need* to be ashamed of that? Are there any other options for the way I *need* to feel about myself?"

"No."

Suffice it to say, when faced with adversity, overcoming your own self-defeating thoughts and behaviors is *not* frequently your initial goal. Your *first thought* is often to force cooperation onto the thing that is not cooperating with you; that *thing* that you tell yourself **NEEDS** to change. You will have to learn to put your initial impulse on hold while you *think again* about who actually **NEEDS** to change.

It's probably **YOU**!

***

Most people are satisfied when their behavior follows a familiar pattern, even if it brings bad results. That pattern typically includes the idea that others who don't follow your point of reason are *wrong*. "Everyone agrees with me, so I must be right. If I'm right, you're wrong. Not only are you wrong, but you are the epitome of shit-headed-ness for being wrong and questioning my right-ness." Options abound, however, when we ***think twice*** and come to realize that there are always additional selections for our first emotional response.

"How dare you say that to me?"

"I will say anything I want to you!"

"I'm afraid you don't care about me."

"I don't."

"Well, that's too bad. We could have been friends."

"We're not. We never will be friends."

"OK, well good luck to you. Although your approval would be nice to have, I don't ***need*** it to live ***hap-i-licious-ly*** in my life."

"Really? You're serious."

"Yup."

"You don't want to fight?"

"Well, maybe for the exercise."

"Bring it."

***

Improving your EI is seemingly like developing a new character and learning a new script. "The ***old me*** used to say this, but, after thinking about it again, the ***new me*** will think this way and do that instead."

As a rule, your *inner dialogue*, your *script* is not readily apparent without first learning how to access your self-talk and learning how to **think twice** about the situation you're facing. You have been the **character** you are playing now for your entire life.

You know your lines so well.

You don't even have to think too much about what to say when you are called on to play a particular role.

The **unhappy customer**.

The **dejected lover**.

The **criticized employee**.

The **angry driver**.

There are times, however, when you are faced with something less familiar. Something happens and you don't quite know what to say or do. I once called for telephone information and asked the operator for help with a phone number. "Yes, Joe Schmo in Kansas City, please."

"It's Christmas Eve," the operator said.

"I know that."

"Well, fuck you then," the operator responded with a little chuckle in her voice.

"What!"

"Fuck you."

"Let me speak to your supervisor!"

She hung up.

I had never heard of anything like this!

I ran through every single rule of **engagement** (and **enragement**) I had ever learned up to that point in my life, to try to understand what was happening. Was I wrong to call for information

59

on Christmas Eve? Did I wake her up? Did I commit some social *faux pas*? Should I have greeted her with my warm **Happy Holidays** character? The one I use to show people I am ***inclusive***? Did she have the right to say that to me? I had no character developed for this role – the ***telephone-information-operator-victim***.

    I called my sister to see if I was sick the day our parents taught us these rules about calling the telephone operator on Christmas Eve. Of course I would be happy to apologize to her if ***I were somehow wrong***! She was one of millions of telephone operators, so I probably wouldn't be able to apologize to **HER**. I could feel ***guilty*** every time I thought about it, though, if it turned out I was wrong. For the moment I satisfied myself with being right . . . and ***angry***.

    "Yeah, she said that to me."

    "What *exactly* was her tone of voice again?"

    "She said, 'Fuck you.' Who cares what her voice sounded like?"

    "I do. It makes a difference."

    "She seemed to be enjoying herself. She giggled after she said it. It was unusual. It was a giggle, grin-frown-smirk-scowl-smile-thing."

    "It sounds like she was trying to flirt."

    "Good lord. What should I have done?"

    "You ***needed*** to tell her off. She ***shouldn't*** be talking on the phone like that."

    "You told me to fuck off on the phone two weeks ago."

    "Yeah, but that's different. Sisters can say that. Operators can't. It's like a universal rule or something. You really are naïve when it comes to these things."

Improving your EI will require that you reason differently – something you wouldn't normally do. By listening to your inner dialogue and impeding your first impulse to do what you have become accustomed to doing, you will be improving your skills. The conversation with my sister, after thinking twice, may have gone like this:

"Yeah, she said that to me."

"What *exactly* was her tone of voice again?"

"She said, 'Fuck you.' Who cares what her voice sounded like?"

"I do. It makes a difference."

"I don't know what it sounded like. It hardly matters. I didn't like it, but it happened and, well, people act foolishly all the time."

"It sounds like she was trying to flirt."

"You know, it's really hard to say. I will never really know, will I? I will just chalk it up to experience. My first response was to make myself angry because I told myself it was awful that a telephone operator would talk to me that way and that I couldn't stand her disrespect. Then I thought about it more. I *can* stand it and I don't *need* her respect to be *hap-i-licious*. I don't think I would behave that way if I were answering the phone for BellSouth, no matter what day it was. But you never really know."

"What the fuck are you talking about? *Hap-i-licious*? Have you lost your mind? You *needed* to tell her off. She *shouldn't* be talking on the phone like that. *Hap-i-licious*?"

"I *needed* this or you *needed* this? Besides, you told me to fuck off two weeks ago on the phone."

"Yeah, but that's different. I'm about to do it again, too. What the fuck is ***hap-i-licious***?"

Nothing can better bring you peace than yourself.

"Events, situations and circumstances hold no natural, intrinsic meaning. We must apply meaning to events, situations and circumstances to bring them to emotional life."

Five – *Where are my emotions?*

I am not surprised anymore to find that so many people are not quite sure where their emotions live.

Think about it.

Where do you store your emotions?

What are your emotions made from?

How do your emotions become your emotions?

I am quite used to hearing, "My emotions are in my heart," or "My emotions are in my stomach." I sometimes hear from people seeking couples counseling who are convinced that their emotions are in their ass. "Well, he's a pain in my ass. My emotions must live there," often followed by, "Yeah, and she is a pain in my neck."

It's best to know a little about where your emotions live before you can logically set your sights on changing them. Otherwise you will find yourself aimlessly wandering about looking for them – chasing your tail, so to speak.

First, emotion does not live in the heart, neck, stomach or, for that matter, your ass.

Emotion lives in your head.

More precisely, emotion lives in your brain. Emotion is a product of a number of electrical, chemical and hormonal interactions within the brain and other anatomical configurations of the body. When you *think*, you release these substances into your brain and a chain reaction occurs. The body's rejoinder to emotional stimuli is only sustained or disrupted by *new* thought, unconsciousness or death.

I can't make it any more romantic than that.

Even when you're in love there is very little evidence that it is a genesis of any mystical, magical or other-worldly influence. It is, sadly, a rush of very enjoyable neurochemicals that can become quite addictive over time. For at least 1 in 5, these chemicals might dissipate, leaving some former lovers wondering what in hell came over them in the first place.

To get a better picture of the electrical, chemical and hormonal interactions that take place in the brain and affect other anatomical configurations of the body, let's imagine ourselves in a real-life, emotionally-charged situation. Let's imagine that you take your purchases to the checkout at the grocery store and the cashier doesn't greet you.

In fact, she hardly notices you.

(Is this familiar to anyone?)

She is too busy talking on her cell phone. (Apparently, as far as you can discern, her boyfriend cheated on her the night before with her sister. "You killed me! You're a complete bastard! You ripped my heart out! You really pissed me off! I am going to beat her senseless!")

The cashier rolls your items over the scanner, pays no attention to anything but the barcode and swears into her cell phone. She pushes a button on the cash register, puts the same finger back in her ear, turns her back to you and shouts into the phone. "You're a bastard! A whore!" You get out your credit card and wait to hand it to her. She finally takes it and swipes it. She tears off your receipt, tosses it onto the counter, but doesn't give you a pen to write your name.

She returns to her call.

You ask for a pen.

With a sigh, she pulls one from behind her ear and slams it down (with an elongated sigh) in front of you. You sign, feeling the grease from the woman's hair on your fingers, and you wonder if she plans to give you a bag to carry out your purchases. She doesn't, so you ask for one. You leave your signed receipt on the counter, put your purchases in a bag yourself and go to your car.

Back at the car, you realize your heart is racing and you can't think clearly. You want a *Hershey's* bar to fuel your racing metabolism. You imagine returning to the store dressed as the Green Hornet and performing a flying scissor heel hook on the cashier. You might even imagine taking her cell phone and smashing it onto the checkered floor tiles and stomping on it with your green boots. You think about writing a letter to the store manager. You give up that idea quickly because the manager is probably stupid and likely doesn't care anyway. You settle for pleasuring yourself with thoughts of the cashier's boyfriend cheating on her again! With the store manager! You determine, after all, that the cashier is **an asshole** – wholly irredeemable, damnable and deserving of utter disrespect. "How dare she treat me with such disregard? She has **no right** to be so rude to me. She **should** know how to behave. Someone *should* train her or fire her or, better yet, hang her! Someone *should* do something!"

You're right.

Let's do something.

****

Human beings are capable of processing only two essential, yet opposing, emotional potentials – *fear* and ***attachment***. In fact, humans (much like other animals) have not evolved these two essential responses to their social environments to meet the demands of our modern world.

- When we are in *balance*, we are expressing attachment.
- When we are *out of balance*, we express fear.

From these two essential emotions we are capable of expressing a magnitude of other ***derivative emotions*** (products of fear and attachment). Anger, depression, fury, rage, irritation and resentment are all ***products of the main emotion – fear***. Joy, delight, elation and happiness are ***products of attachment***.

When we are at *rest* and in balance (available for attachment with others) our perceived world is stable, unfettered. People are normally in balance when they are not making themselves worried, angry or thinking threatening thoughts. Reading this book, for example, may be a time of balance for you. You might be lying in bed, giggling at doing a flying scissor heel hook lock on the cashier, relaxed. If you are not in balance while reading this book, it probably makes no sense at all to be reading it. You should close it and come back later. People don't often think clearly when they're in a state of *fear*.

The *fear* response might be better described as your ***stress response*** or your ***fight, flight*** or ***freeze response***.

"I am really pissed!"

"What are you afraid of?"

"Afraid! I'm not afraid of that bitch. She *makes* me so mad though."

"How is her behavior a problem for you?"

"She thinks she is so perfect."

"What would it mean if she thought she were perfect?"

"It would mean she was judging me."

"How is that a problem for you?"

"I'm not perfect."

"Yeah, that's a pretty scary notion."

Our two natural emotional potentials, **attachment** and *fear*, have remained, fundamentally, un-evolved since they were gifted by Nature to our prehistoric ancestors.

Every emotion we express is a derivative of fear or attachment.

We are, unfortunately, stuck with an emotional response system that does not suit our modern age. We continue to view events within our perception as either *threatening* or *nonthreatening*.

Instead of wildebeests, blobfish and yeti crabs, our modern-day threats are traffic jams, cashiers, disagreements, pedophiles, bills, jobs and our own ego weaknesses.

Sitting quietly in your back yard, for instance, enjoying a midsummer evening with your partner is often *nonthreatening* and quite enjoyable.

Balanced.

A disagreement over how much your partner likes your new hairstyle can be perceived much the same way as you would perceive a blobfish attack – a disruption to your homeostatic balance. Suddenly you are feeling ***threatened***.

"How dare you criticize my hair?"

"I'm just sayin'."

"What am I going to do now? You ruined our whole night."

"How did I do that?"

"You said my hair made me look older."

"How is looking older a problem for you?"

"You shouldn't talk to me that way. You should always love everything about me. You should never criticize me. You should treat me kindly all the time. Even if you have to lie to me."

"So what did it mean when I said I didn't like your haircut?"

"It meant that you HATE me!"

"What would it mean if I hated you?"

"Don't get me started."

Telling your partner you don't like h/er haircut is ***benign unto itself***. Your partner gave meaning to your observation and ***behaved*** according to h/er thoughts. You partner could have chosen to respond from a state of attachment, but, it appears in this case, the response was built from fear. The factor that makes h/er emotional reaction h/er ***own doing*** is that s/he perceived your comment as ***threatening***. S/he generated thoughts and expressed those thoughts as emotion. In this case, s/he may have chosen to react in defense of h/er ego. "If I am criticized, I am a failure. I cannot have that. I must protect myself from that implication."

Events, situations and circumstances hold no ***natural, intrinsic meaning***. We must apply meaning to events, situations and circumstances to bring them to emotional life.

Without perception and meaning, there is no emotional life.

For example, the quickest, most foolproof way to discover the ***meaning*** behind your anger is to ***ask yourself what you are afraid of***.

"My husband doesn't like my hairstyle. What am I afraid of? Well, if he doesn't like my hairstyle, no one else will like it. If no one likes my hairstyle, they will ridicule me. They won't like me. If I am ridiculed, I will be a bad person. If I am a bad person, I have no real function in society. If that were the case, goodness, I wouldn't have any value at all! I better get a hairstyle that pleases *everyone*. That way I will retain my value as a human being."

If you are honest with yourself, you will discover a multitude of answers that will help you get in touch with resolving your fear / anger response. Capturing your thoughts can provide you with ample opportunity to do something about your emotions. "I am being criticized. I am ***angry***. What am I ***afraid*** of? I am afraid that if I am criticized I am not appreciated for my intelligence. If I am not appreciated for my intelligence, I will be viewed as stupid. If I am viewed as stupid, I must be stupid. ATTACK of the yeti crabs!"

The fact is, you can be called stupid all day and you *can* stand it. People might truly believe you are stupid, ugly, fat, rude and unfriendly. The significance of those words is only as useful as your personal assessment of them. As previously stated, you are not likely to enjoy it when you are criticized. You can, undoubtedly, live ***hap-i-licious-ly*** with people who don't celebrate the high opinion you hold of yourself.

"You disgust me."

"Prove it."

"You know, you are really stupid."

"I guess you'll just have to find a way to live with that."

"You'll never change! You're the same as you have ever been."

"Don't judge me by my past; I don't live there anymore."

****

We are not often threatened anymore by wild animals.

We are still quit susceptible, however, to perceiving threats to our emotional balance (threats our mind often perceives as threats to our physical safety). Our balance often depends on maintaining a solid foundation for who we believe ourselves to be. Balance is often disrupted when that perception is being scrutinized. When there is **ANY KIND OF THREAT** to you, be it an actual physical threat or a threat to your idea of yourself as a parent, a neighbor, a softball pitcher, a poll dancer, a McDonald's cashier, a citizen, a Democrat, a glass blower – it is all perceived in much the same way as you would respond to any threat – with a *fight, flight* or *freeze response*. Nature does, however, allow for great flexibility in how we perceive threats. After all, *emotional flexibility is the key principle* and core advantage we have in improving our EI.

Personality is very plastic.

If it weren't, we wouldn't be having this discussion. Instead I would be trying to help you learn to live better with your unalterable, irreversible insanity.

****

How we use our arms and legs to navigate the world is as important as how we use our personalities when we get to where we're going. As we ambulate from one place to another, from one culture to the next, our personalities are quite plastic, malleable and infinitely expandable to meet the expectations of the people we encounter.

Nature provides for that potential because we must, as human beings, as I previously suggested, *cooperate, congregate* and *copulate* no matter where we find ourselves. Without this impulse to demonstrate recognizable social behavior, our species would not adapt and would, instead, go extinct.

Because Nature has no idea where a human being will be born or to whom, the human personality is purposefully made flexible, adaptable to anywhere we grow and develop. Survival depends on the individual's innate agility for assimilation. Just as important is our human capacity to acquire thinking and corresponding behaviors that further that purpose.

Our emotional life would be much more predictable and less threatening if we all simply grew up in one great big household, learned the very same *rules of engagement* (and enragement) and never left there. We would all, in simple terms, understand one another, our motives, our beliefs, our standards of good and bad. But we don't all grow up around the same system of evaluation. We have to leave home and the minute we do, we encounter challenge to what we think we know about the *rules* of human interaction. If truth be told, there are no rules except to *cooperate, congregate* and *copulate* as much like everyone else as possible. The rest we make up inside our own heads.

"I wasn't raised like that;"

"My parents taught me to be polite. You need to be polite;"

"People should treat me with respect;"

"YOU DON'T KNOW HOW TO BEHAVE!"

EI theory is partially a product of the idea that **PEOPLE MUST LIVE IN A LARGER SOCIETY**. We don't often grow up only to live in our own backyards. If we did, we may be more content.

It is not likely that we can change the broad spectrum of society to resemble our own backyards. There may be as many as 3.5 billion different households that would be vying for the top spot. We can, however, recognize that our personalities are flexible enough to assimilate to nearly any unique household, community or culture we encounter. We can accommodate 3.5 billion households, if we *want* to do that. With proper guidance, anyone can take advantage of that potential.

Learning new ways of behaving is essential to survival.

If, for example, you were to suddenly find yourself living in a tribe of head hunters, and your survival depended on adapting to that culture, you would have a great deal of potential for assimilating. The *plastic nature* of your personality makes that goal quite achievable. This concept is what gives EI its immense advantage. You can change, refashion, remodel, or maintain the way you think about threats to your **beliefs, archetypes** and **models of right** and **wrong**.

This philosophy does not mean you have to give up the cherished lessons taught to you by your family, your respected elders, your heroes, your friends and teachers.

On the contrary.

It means that you can make little adjustments to your strongly held beliefs by adding the concept that people **DO NOT** have to believe the same things you do in order for you to live *hap-i-licious-ly* with them. People do not have to behave according to your rules in order to achieve a healthy level of cooperation. People can behave any way they choose.

Just like you do.

Hold on to your honorable beliefs, values, morals and standards for emotive behavior. Your beliefs may one day be the standards by which our culture is judged. In the meantime, you will have to make room for those who do not think the same way you do – for people who didn't grow up in your household, in your community or, seemingly, your universe. You simply have to recognize the potential of your thinking and take advantage of its *flexibility*.

****

The *fight, freeze* or *flee* response is a bit more complicated than just changing the way we think. The fact is, when we think, we trigger a flood of electro-neuro-chemical-hormonal response that stimulate us to prepare for aggression. Remember, we are prepared to fight, freeze or flee regardless of the threat. A polar bear and a poorly-behaving cashier are perceived in much the same way by the brain – as threats.

Your brain's automatic response to your perception of threat is to trigger an electro- neuro-chemical-hormonal defense response – messages sent from the brain (the limbic system) to the pituitary gland that instigate a reaction from such things as your heart, lungs, digestion, kidneys, skin, hair and cooling response (perspiration).

That's why, when you are making yourself angry, your heart beats faster, you get a hot jolt of heat up the back of your neck, your face perspires and you have to pee. All of these responses are necessary for preparing you for and sustaining your response to threat. You might, for example, have the same or similar perception of a wild, rabid dog and your perception of a cashier who is behaving counter to your expectations. The more you perceive danger, the more your body will prepare itself for fighting, fleeing or freezing.

The only way to inhibit that phenomenon, once it has started, is to either ***think differently*** or ***wait*** for the chemicals to dissipate. (It may be best when you return to your car after your encounter with the cashier to wait for the chemical rush to take its course. Breathe deeply and slowly. Breathing deeply stimulates the ***vagus nerve*** and sends messages to the brain that the threat is no longer present and that your body can begin the process of returning to a state of balance.)

Waiting, alone, for the chemicals to run their course, without some level of cognitive interference, can last from seconds to the rest of your life. If you are making yourself chronically stressed, you may have trained your body to respond to the world in this very apprehensive, defensive manner all the time.

You might view everything within your perception as threatening.

This is the nature of ***post-traumatic stress***. After prolonged exposure to a real or imagined threat, the brain will take steps to protect itself from nearly everything – any external stimulus becomes a potential threat. Over time, a state of traumatic stress may develop, making progress in improving EI slow and burdensome – but still very possible.

Regardless, it seems to me that once people get the hang of knowing where their emotions live, how their emotions are related to thinking and what happens to the body when the body is in a ***state of action***, people are more likely to zero in on where they should begin the process of emotional problem-solving and improving their EI.

NOTE: I mentioned in an earlier chapter that people are more likely to respond to the question, "What are you telling yourself?" if they are in an expansive, happy state of mind. We wondered why that exercise is so troubling for people who are making themselves angry. Simply, when people are in a state of stress, or *fight, flight or freeze* and can't easily, quickly or patiently get in touch with the thoughts they are having. People in this frame of mind are focused on protecting themselves from threat and are not easily coaxed into letting their emotional defensiveness down.

Focusing on threat is responsible for the ***thought cycling you experience*** (thinking about the same thing over and over) when you face something you perceive as threatening. Your boss criticizes you. Your wife doesn't like your cooking. Your child tells you s/he hates you. You go to bed and wake up with the same disturbing thoughts.

Asking someone to tell you what they're thinking when they are focused on fear is much like asking someone to tell you what they are thinking as they run through the frozen tundra being chased by a polar bear. It is best, therefore, to relax before you practice your EI skills.

Just concentrate on breathing and relaxing.

If you are focused and committed to change, the rest will come.

Nothing can better bring you peace than yourself.

"Essentially, shit happens and you apply meaning to it. The more meaning you apply to shit the stronger your emotional connection to shit will be."

Six – *Your emotional neighborhood*

We have come approximately seventy-five pages and you might be seriously questioning your emotional motivations, asking yourself if it is indeed true that your emotions are a product of your experiences and thinking.

If you are, that's a good sign.

Your emotional thinking is, for the most part, a product of your experiences. You spend the first twenty-five years of your life learning from your caregivers, your culture and from various other sources how to respond to nearly anything that is likely to occur in that particular culture over a lifetime. Your full appreciation for the rules of cooperation, congregation and copulation take shape during these formative years.

You are a member of society.

"When someone dies, this is how you behave. No exceptions."

"When you are in love, this is how you should express it. No exceptions."

"When someone shows you disrespect, this is what you do. No exceptions."

And you repeat that thinking and its corresponding behavior over and over, to the approval and applause of your teachers, until your thinking becomes indistinguishable from your emotional response. And you come to believe that your emotions are just natural responses to stimuli and that everyone responds (or is expected to respond) the same way to the same or similar stimuli.

"OK, now run along. You're ready for the world."

Your thoughts become your emotions.

From then on, preventing damage to established beliefs seems to take precedence over everything else.

"You said this, and it means that. No exceptions."

"You shouldn't act this way, you should act that way. No exceptions."

"I am a rotten, good-for-nothing scoundrel because I failed. No exceptions."

"I am good and you are bad. No exceptions."

The tricky part is, when you begin to think twice, and settle on a new emotional response, you are, essentially, compromising your learned response. In essence, you are questioning the lessons taught to you by your grandfathers, your mother and your respected neighbors on how to behave with others.

"If someone does this, you should punch them in the eye. No exceptions."

"If you do that, people should always do this. No exceptions."

"People must say please and thank you or they are rude and should be punished. No exceptions."

You might find yourself, now, second-guessing everything you believed to be true and factual about yourself and others. "I know I wasn't taught to behave that way, but this person apparently wasn't. Before I learned to think twice, I would have just pulled this person's spine out through their eye socket. Now, although I would like it more if I were treated nicer, I know I can live without this person's respect and courtesy. I may not be as content as I would be if s/he were showing me courtesy and respect – but I can live contentedly, nonetheless, without it. Instead of being angry, I think I will be sad that this person seems to be acting so carelessly toward me."

****

I would like to emphasize that whatever alternative emotional response you settle on, that emotion MUST BE an alternative you are willing to accept. If forgiveness isn't something you, at this point in your learning, are willing or capable of exchanging for anger, you might think twice about setting forgiveness as an emotional goal. You might seek, instead, something YOU ARE WILLING TO ACCEPT AS A REPLACEMENT.

It isn't that you couldn't express forgiveness in the face of disrespectful or discourteous behavior. Like I said, you may not, at this point in your learning, be capable at this stage in your learning. So, if you're not capable or willing to set forgiveness as an ALTERNATIVE emotional goal, you may look elsewhere for other emotional options. You just may have to settle on sadness, pardoning the behavior, viewing the person as emotionally handicapped or just being less angry.

The key is that if your goal is to improve your emotional intelligence, you must take steps to express some alternative emotional response, other than the one you are accustomed to expressing.

ANYTHING! For now, it truly doesn't matter what emotion you settle on in exchange for your traditional response. It just matters that you take an active role in managing your unmanageable emotions.

Remember, without some adjustment in your definition of happiness, as you endeavor to evolve your emotions, it may not be possible to set happiness as an alternative to anger or rage. In fact, happiness may even be, at this point in your learning, out of reach in instances where you are experiencing annoyance or irritation. You may just have to set your mind to achieving less anger, decreased annoyance, reduced irritation or some form of contentment. Happiness as an emotional response to adversity is a possibility for you. It will just take a lot of time and practice to replace strong, noxious learned emotional responses with any definition of happiness.

Finally, as you progress toward EI improvement, you might, at times, even miss the target altogether. You may simply respond to adversity in your old, familiar way. There is still an opportunity for EI improvement. You can forgive yourself for responding contrary to your EI goals. You can plan to do better next time. You can use this time for practice and rehearsal.

Incremental change, as long as it is self-enhancing and likely to lead to a better emotional result at some point in your goal for improved EI is a magnificent sign of progress.

****

I mentioned previously that thinking twice is sometimes not easy when you are in an emotionally threatening situation. Committing to *thinking twice*, once your body returns to some semblance of *balance* is essential. To return to balance, as stated previously, you will have to either *wait* or *think differently* about the perceived threat. We will try to slow down that process, to better understand the system from an anatomical perspective.

There are a number of brain structures that can be identified as the *physical homes* of emotion. The *limbic system*, a region located approximately in the center of the brain, can be viewed as your *emotional neighborhood*. The limbic system consists of a series of interconnected brain structures that includes the *frontal area* of the brain, the *hippocampus*, *amygdala*, *hypothalamus (anterior thalamic nuclei)*, *septum*, *limbic cortex* and *fornix*. It is believed that these structures support a variety of functions including *emotional behavior* and the *long-term memory* related to emotional behavior. It is **NOT** essential for you, the learner, to know these structures to any great extent – although it could benefit you. Knowing that there are anatomical, electro-bio-chemical and hormonal correlations between your emotions and your brain is, however, critical to improving your EI. Although you may decide not to know these structures, you will have to remember where your emotions live – at minimum. You will be visiting the *limbic neighborhood* a lot, as you endeavor to improve your EI.

It is best to know your neighbors.

The limbic neighborhood, when in balance, can be described as *resting* – but has the *potential* to come alive at any moment in an all-out effort to protect the body from real or perceived harm or threat of harm. This *automatic response* (which means it happens without your consent) involves the release of neurochemicals and hormones into the body that are intent on protecting you from your perceived threat. You can expect a sudden increase in heart rate, perspiration, flushing of the skin, hair standing on end, etc. All designed by Nature to give you the strength, energy and focus to run away very quickly or fight very bravely (or just to freeze, motionless, in the hopes you will appear unthreatening to your attacker).

Let's find a more familiar image to understand this phenomenon.

Imagine that you cut your finger.

Blood flows from your cut, **no matter how much you are against that from happening**.

It is automatic.

The blood flows until it either stops on its own or you *commit* to do something to stop it yourself. If you *commit* to attending to the cut, you might wash it, put it in your mouth or cover it with a Band-Aid (or plaster). Your effort to stop the bleeding will likely shorten the time the wound is active. While attending to the cut, you tell yourself how to avoid such accidents with your bo-staff in the future.

The essential factors in this scenario is that the blood flowed **without your consent**; and it will continue to flow until you *commit* to do something about it; you took reasonable steps to stop it, and you committed to better handling the same or similar type of danger in the future.

We can use this same analogy to better understand what happens when you make yourself angry, depressed, enraged or infuriated.

Of course, the whole process begins with perception and thought.

"I am being disrespected and I cannot stand it!"

That thought is interpreted by the brain as a threat to your wellbeing and begins the *automatic* flow of neurochemicals and hormones into the bloodstream, flooding major organs, activating the flight or freeze (stress) response.

- the heart rate and blood pressure increase;
- the pupils dilate to take in as much light as possible;
- the veins in skin constrict to send more blood to major muscle groups;
- blood-glucose level increases;
- the muscles tense up, energized by adrenaline and glucose;
- the smooth muscle relaxes in order to allow more oxygen into the lungs;
- the digestion and immune system shut down to allow more energy for emergency functions; and
- trouble focusing on small tasks because the brain is focused on big picture in order to determine where threat is coming from.

Like blood from a cut, the flow of neurochemicals and hormones happens without your consent. Like tending to a wound, you must *commit* to providing your thinking with immediate attention. Applying *new thinking*, thinking twice, is much like putting a Band-Aid over the wound.

Keep in mind that the stress response was only designed by Nature to last as long as it took to manage the threat. Traditionally, no more than thirty to forty-five seconds. Your stress response was not designed to last days, months and years. Prolonged exposure to the neurochemicals and hormones that activate the stress response burdens vital organs, i.e., heart, liver, kidneys, adrenal glands, etc. that are taxed with pumping these dangerous chemicals through your body. These substances will also begin to deteriorate your body's major organs, resulting in a number of compromising health problems, e.g., heart disease, obesity, a weakened immune system, muscle, joint, skin and stomach problems.

It is best to apply that Band-aid to your thinking, as soon as possible, to prevent whole-body infection.

EI is a process of **commitment** to **conscious negotiation** with the quiet neighbors, the aggressive neighbors and the mediator who all live together in the **limbic neighborhood**. Suffice it to say that more often than not, before you emote (have emotions) you **think**. There are few exceptions to this rule. It is your second thought, when you choose to **think twice**, that your EI will intercede in the negotiations and help settle on a more self-preserving, less aggressive response to disturbances to your balance.

Nothing can better bring you peace than yourself.

"Sanity is a concept."

"Really?"

"Yes, really. Do you know what I mean by a concept?"

"When you put it that way, I'm not sure."

"It means sanity doesn't exist without imagination."

Seven – *What in the hell was I thinking?*

This may be a good opportunity to introduce **the first** of the *problem-solving methods* we will be using to improve our EI:

- **Commitment** to change

Committing to change is dependent on **really, truly believing** that you always think before you feel emotion. That ***idea*** will have to become a *fact* for you, before you can successfully commit to changing your **conditioned emotional response** and improving your emotional intelligence using this theory.

It is essential to get in touch with your first thought in order to learn to think twice. Remember, however, that recognizing that you are thinking **SOMETHING**, and making the decision to change the way you are thinking *in the moment* will likely be the tough part (especially in the midst of an emotional crisis).

Don't despair.

No matter what happens, what you think or how that effort seems far-fetched and out of your control, committing to change is your only goal at this point. Telling yourself that you are not managing your emotions in a manner that is bringing you good results takes effort – effort to which most people are not often willing to commit. Regardless, the suggestions from here on will be useless unless you **commit to emotional improvement** – commit to **thinking twice**.

In addition to committing to change, we will begin to improve our emotional with:

- **Problem identification** (PI) and
- Discouraging **emotional conformity and** encouraging **emotional range**

Emotional struggles often surface without any notice at all. We frequently find ourselves working within the framework of our *first thoughts* without even realizing it. Suddenly it's too late and those neurochemicals and hormones we discussed previously are racing through our bodies, focusing our attention on the *perceived threat* rather than making a rational choice to impede the automatic response and **think twice**.

We have long trained our brains to think only once and settle on that limited perspective to address the issues we face. It will take a lot of time and practice to be fast enough to begin **thinking twice**, while in the middle of emotional chaos. Until your skills are refined, I can suggest that you pay attention to your thoughts and how your body is responding to them.

And breathe!

Without the benefit of hearing our first thoughts, we cannot begin to make progress toward **commitment to change** and **problem identification**.

I am never amazed anymore, after asking my learners what brings them in to see me that they really don't know. They just **NEED** to talk to someone. People seem to **NEED** to reach outside themselves before they even try to reach inside for their answers.

Voila! The impetus for the mental health therapist.

Of course, people do *imagine* they know what brings them to see a therapist. It is soon clear, however, that their imagination has gotten the worst of them.

"I want to talk about how my mother *makes* me depressed."

"How do you know you're depressed?"

"Well, my mother treats me like a child and I don't like it."

"How is that a problem for you?"

"I don't like to be treated like a child. I'm sixteen years old. I should be treated like an adult."

"What does it mean if your mother treats you like a child?"

"It means I will *never* grow up and I will never be an adult."

"That isn't likely, but what if that happened?"

"I would never be able to have a family or get a job or be independent."

"Goodness, what would it mean if you didn't get to do all that?"

"I would be a *loser*. People would think I was a failure."

"I can understand now what you mean. Telling oneself all that nutty stuff might just lead to depression. Or maybe some heavy-duty sadness. I think, before we talk about your mother's behavior, we might spend a little time talking about you and your *imaginative thoughts*. We can leave your mother for another time. How does that sound?"

"Yes, I'm willing to do that."

****

Problem identification (PI) is the next step, after ***committing to change***. Let's begin our discovery of PI using a common social construct – *disrespect*.

Disrespect, insolence, impertinence (however you may want to identify this phenomenon) is common at, of all places, the checkout counter. (You'd think that places of business that rely on customer satisfaction would be the *last* place you would experience such a phenomenon. I should note that I have never met a more gracious group of dedicated employees than those who are employed by the *Apple Store*.) Let's use the scenario with the grocery store cashier from Chapter Five as our model for this exercise.

It is not uncommon these days to find ourselves expecting to be treated as a customer, only to find we are being *perceived* as more of a *nuisance*. Our experience with the cashier in Chapter Five is an example of one of those times when we are *not getting cooperation* from people we believe *should* cooperate with us.

In order to begin to make better sense of this circumstance, our first goal is to recognize that our *limbic neighborhood* was activated by our perception – our *first thought* – of danger. The cashier, for all intents and purposes, suddenly became a black bear right before our eyes.

Remember: *Some bear attacks begin with a polite knock at the door*.

Prepare for them.

Without much notice, your body will go into action to fuel the protective response to *your perception of danger*.

That first jolt of electric fear travels through your body and prepares you for fighting, fleeing or freezing. It is not likely that you would have been very successful at changing anything about that initial jolt. It happened before you could do anything about it.

It's like blood from a cut.

It's automatic.

You might use this opportunity to pay attention for a moment or two and become more familiar with what is going on in your mind and in your body.

Breathe!

VERY deeply.

When you are ready to *commit to thinking twice*, you will be taking your first step toward *discouraging emotional conformity*. You will be committing to using the *flexibility* of your *emotional range*.

You will do something else!

Something you don't normally do.

****

- Begin by first finding a *quiet place.* Somewhere you can be alone. Often, I find that the car is a good place for this activity – but turn off the radio. If you have a spare room in your home that you can use to privately *think twice*, go there. You will need privacy while you begin the process of *identifying the problem* (PI).
- PI starts with simply re-telling oneself *precisely* what happened.

- Problem identification requires the unfamiliar behavior of speaking the problem out loud – *articulated thought*. That's one of the reasons for all the solitude and quite. Unless you're comfortable talking to yourself in a super market or on the bus, your selection of a private, *not public*, spot will help you achieve this purposeful goal. (If you simply cannot find a quite place, and you want to begin this process immediately, pull out your cell phone and start talking on it. No one will know the difference.)
- **NOTE**: It may be a good idea, *before* starting this process of articulating thought, to simply hear your own voice. Talk to yourself, out loud. The experience can be both amazing and, at the same time, confusing.
- You may consider articulating thought even before going into problem-identification mode. On your way home from work, prison or the grocery store, simply say: "Hello there! We have known each other all our lives and we have never once talked to each other in private. I want to be successful at improving my emotional intelligence, so I am going to try out this technique."
- Hear your own voice. That way, when the time comes that you will rely on yourself to help solve your own emotional problems the sound of your own voice won't be such a surprise. You might say, after introducing yourself to yourself, "It has been nice meeting you. Let's plan to talk every day."
- *Articulated thought* is intended to help you stay focused on the details of what you are experiencing or have experienced.

(You are less likely to exaggerate or lie to yourself for obvious reasons, as well.)

- Thinking *alone* has a tendency to result in a loss of concentration. If you only *think* about what concerns you, your mind may wander and, before you know it, you may lose track of your problem-solving goal and be less focused.
- *Articulate thought as if you were telling your story to a friend*, only stick with the facts.
- Avoid *embellishment, exaggeration, hyperbole, amplification* and *overstatement*.
- Verbalize an *accurate and clear description of the event that concerns you.*
- Do not amplify using words like *very, a lot, extremely, awful, horrible* or *incredibly*. Simply describe the event as it truly happened.
- Don't imagine that you know what anyone else is thinking. *State only the facts* as they would be observed by someone who was watching but had no stake in the outcome.
- For example: I walked up to the cash register with my purchases. The cashier was on the phone. She was swearing and shouting. She turned her back to me. She gave me a receipt. I asked for a pen. She gave me a pen. It had some sort of greasy substance on it. She didn't give me a bag. I bagged my purchases and left the store.
- After describing the event, ask yourself *what about this event is a problem for you*.
- Say out loud, *"How was this event a problem for me?"*

- As you endeavor to answer this question, you might pay special attention to how you use the words *should, ought, must, have to* and *need*. You may also pay attention to your use of the words *awful, horrible* and *the idea that you can't stand it*. For example:
- "It's a problem for me because I was treated badly and I *should* not ever be treated badly – especially when it is intentionally."
- "It's a problem for me because I *need* people to treat me with respect if I am going to be happy in my life."
- "It's a problem for me because I *must* have the respect of others (including strangers) if I am going to be happy."
- "It's a problem for me because people should treat me respectfully."
- "If I am treated disrespectfully, it is *awful, horrible* and *I cannot stand it*."
- After articulating the event and asking yourself how the circumstance was a problem for you, a more *accurate description of the problem* will begin to surface and take on an altogether-different dimension.
- The problem will, in fact, become something you can actually do something about. You will begin to focus on yourself and your own ability to do something about your own emotional problems.
- **New Problem**: "This problem has nothing to do with the cashier and everything to do with me and the way I think whenever I perceive that I am being disrespected. When I am treated disrespectfully, I tell myself *I shouldn't be* treated that

way; I *need* respect from everyone I meet, and I *cannot stand it* when I don't get it."

- *Voila*! The problem suddenly becomes *yours and yours alone*. More importantly, the solution to the problem becomes much more possible than it would have been if you attributed your feelings to someone or something outside your control. If the problem is with the way you think, **YOU** can change the emotional outcome.

****

We will discuss the *solution process* in the coming chapters. I would like to assure my learner, however, that *acknowledging your role* in how you make yourself feel does not intend to condone, ignore or overlook noxious behavior. Noxious behavior is not (and likely will never be) enjoyable, pleasing or agreeable to you. It is not our goal to have you reward noxious behavior. Nor is it our goal to have you give a positive response to noxious behavior (although you could do that). It is our goal to encourage you to accept that noxious behavior exists, NO MATTER HOW MUCH YOU DEMAND THAT IT DOESN'T, that you can live your life *hap-i-licious-ly* in a world where adversity does exist and that you are more likely to help people hear your point of view if you are in a more rational frame of mind – *if* you decide to express your opinion. (This condition comes in handy when you are making yourself feel disagreeable toward people with whom you have a prolonged commitment. You may want to be in a better, more welcoming frame of mind when expressing your preferences to your husband, wife, partner, coworkers or children. You may not wish to do so when you are making yourself angry with a grocery store clerk – although you could. It's really up to you.)

****

I would like to offer a suggestion only for the ***very focused and intent emotional intelligence learner***. (This exercise is not for the faint of heart and takes a total commitment to emotional growth.) I suggest that your ***early*** articulated thoughts begin with a self introduction – much like meeting someone new. Try this dialogue with yourself:

- "Hello (your name). I have known you all my life, but I have never taken the time to meet you and get to know you. We spend all day together, and I hardly know you. You are the only person I can truly trust with my emotional growth. You are my best friend. We will spend the rest of our life together, and we will rely on our best judgment to make the best possible emotional decisions. I want to commit to talking with you every day, as I drive home from work and review my day. If it seems we had an emotional problem, we can use the ***EI articulated thought paradigm*** to solve it. Talk with you tomorrow.

****

The EI articulated thought theory is intended to provide you with some relief from the way you make yourself feel when people *choose* to behave unpleasantly toward you. People have an inalienable right to express themselves any way they choose. Your task is to acknowledge that fact and make a better adjustment than you are used to making. Once you have successfully completed the first steps in this process –discouraging ***emotional conformity***, encouraging ***emotional range*** and ***problem identification*** – the resultant problem will be sitting squarely in **YOUR** lap. You can then face the challenge of changing your perception to one that will likely lead to your own *emotional evolution*.

Nothing can better bring you peace than yourself.

*"The idea that people treat you unfortunately is **only meaningful** if **you** place some level of significance on it and make some sort of inference about it."*

Eight – *The burden of change is on you*

Your emotional issues are not normally related to any particular event or circumstance. Your emotions are more likely a result of how *you perceive* an event or circumstance. ***Incidents, circumstances, situations and events are meaningless until you give them meaning.*** If you are going to make any kind of progress in improving your EI, it will be essential to ***properly identify*** the problem you are facing and then ***recognize the role perception and thought play*** in how you settle on an emotional response.

Too often, even when working with a professional therapist, identifying the problem is not the primary goal. A professional EI guide, however, may ask, after hearing what the learner thinks is h/er problem, "How is it a problem for you?" intentionally placing the ***burden of change on the learner***, purposefully removing others from the problem-solving adventure. (The idea that people treat you unfortunately is ***only meaningful*** if ***you*** place some level of significance on it and make some sort of inference about it.)

****

Rather than thinking other people have to change *their* behavior in order for you to be happy in life, you will learn that the problem and the solution will not rely on the cooperation of anyone but **YOU** to resolve it. The cashier we discussed in previous chapters can continue to behave as she pleases. (She, likely, has her own problems.) You, on the other hand, will be driving home in your car, articulating your thoughts, making active, conscious decisions to *think twice* about what the problem TRULY is and what you intend to do to change it. That way, when you get to the *second strategy*, you will be ready to perceive measureable change in your EI.

Keep in mind that if you fail at your initial attempts at defining your *true problem*, it's not the end of the line.

Don't give up!

There are a few more steps in this process that we will consider.

Identifying your problem and owning it is your present goal.

Problem identification takes a lot of skill, dexterity in thought and practice. (You can email me at Michael.Cornwall@eitheory.com or visit my blog at http://www.eitheory.com and I will help you, if you have *really* tried and can't do it!) Granted, developing expertise in these initial steps in EI theory (especially articulated thought) is time-consuming. You can expect to have difficulty with some part of it.

Forgive yourself!

Besides, your biggest leap of faith is not going to be articulated thought. It will be admitting to yourself that you want to *own your problems* (rather than attributing them to others) and then *committing* to that goal. For more information on *identifying the problem* and

improving emotional range, see the section of this book marked **Sample Sessions**.

Nothing can better bring you peace than yourself.

"The fact that you or anyone else treats you disrespectfully is scarcely enough evidence to induce panic."

Nine: *Peach Ice Cream*

We must *perceive* before we can emote.

We must perceive that we are perceiving, before we can perceive differently.

We must learn to think about our thinking.

Perception is a combination of mental and physical processes involving individual *experience, hearing, seeing, touching, tasting* and *smelling*. For example, if a person is unconscious, s/he will not be disturbed by a grizzly bear eating grapes off h/er chest. If the individual suddenly awakes, however, within nanoseconds, perceptual information is immediately gathered. It passes swiftly through the brain, much like electricity, is translated into neuro-signals and results in the instantaneous distribution of those sticky, gooey substances we talked about earlier, travelling at the speed of light throughout the body, preparing it for running, fighting, freezing or some combination of all three.

This is the perception of FEAR! and its corollaries. It will be important to remember that this stress response – this fight, flight or freeze reaction is identical to the response you have to noxious interactions with others. Realizing that your emotions are produced by your *perception of events* – by your thinking and your body's electro-chemical-hormonal response to thinking is *essential* to improving your EI.

***

Suffice it to say, discussing humans as *animals* driven by *instinct* is a delicate issue. People often like to view themselves as somehow more than woodland creatures. That is an honorable ambition. As we progress to a fuller understanding of emotional intelligence, however, the evidence for our purpose as a species will become more compelling. In the meantime, we will bask in our glory as the kings of the jungle. At any rate, we owe our *limited* emotional range (attachment and fear) to *Nature*. We can attribute our *broader* assortment of emotions (anger, sadness, joy, disappointment, happiness and depression) to learning, experience and *imagination*.

This is where *simplification* of EI theory gets complicated.

Grab your canoe.

Over time (about 276,000 years), our human species was gifted with two essential, yet conflicting emotional potentials – *fear* and *attachment*. Fundamentally, we possess the ability to communicate *fear* in situations where we are being threatened and *attachment* in most situations that are not perceived as threatening. (There are actually times when humans will express fear in the form of attachment behaviors when they are being threatened. But that is entirely another issue.)

Fear and *attachment* are your fundamental, crucial human emotional potentials. All other emotions, i.e., sadness, joy, anger and happiness are *derivative* of these two necessary basics and are uniquely expressed by your primary culture. You might say that the emotions you use every day were learned through experience and are simply gradations or degrees of fear and attachment.

The expression of *love* (a derivative of attachment), for instance, is often difficult to describe, universally. There are as many distinctive definitions of love as there are people. An individual who is reared in an environment where violence is used as a prelude to expressing affection may seek a partner who can accommodate that definition. S/he may raise h/er children the same way, thereby illustrating the example that emotion is best understood within a particular family / community culture.

A primary caregiver who shows enthusiastic support of a child's development by feeding, changing, responding to cries, cuddling and playing, will teach the child to recognize the unique character of *attachment behavior* within that particular culture. From these experiences, the child may learn how to recognize joy, happiness, contentment, forgiveness and delight – each a derivative of the essential emotion *attachment*.

This very simplified discussion of fear and attachment and its derivatives is intended to provide my learner with a clearer appreciation for the origin of their emotions – what's natural (fear and attachment) and what is wo/manmade (everything else) – building on the concept that emotion is primarily a product of repeated exposure to *thought* and *experience*. This understanding is essential to appreciate the idea that if the emotion is created by the mind it can be uncreated by the mind.

****

Although the breadth and width of our emotional range is boundless, we remain inherently tribal, most adept in family or small community units (herds), driven by an instinct to ***cooperate, congregate*** and ***copulate***.

But we really don't live in our families of origin and small familiar communities much anymore. In fact, we often grow up and soon venture into a world where we encounter others whose emotional learning experiences are at odds with our own. In small tribes or communities, we could regulate behavior through such social controls as shunning, mockery, ostracization and expulsion. In the case of the cashier in the grocery store, for instance, we could, if we lived in small groups, threaten to tell her mother on her if she doesn't behave. Now, unless the social behavior affects enough people, our world is often too large for such threats. Modern wo/man has come together to live in larger communities but, the shock of diversity in emotional upbringing has forced us to live quietly alone, fearful of unpredictable social encounters, frustrating ourselves when looking for ways to address our experiences with noxious experiences with others.

We have lost the ability to anticipate one another.

As our world cultures collide, mesh and repel, conflict results over what is right and what is wrong, good and bad, best and better. Individuality (rather than communal living) is now the key to a ***long*** and rewarding life.

And we do live so much longer now.

Since the discovery of fire, we have met the challenges of Nature with more success, preserving and propagating our species with each subsequent discovery. In our quest to survive, however, we've placed ourselves and our mental health under a *measured threat*.

Simply, we have weakened our emotional intelligence.

We build fast and expensive cars, receive Academy awards, erect fences, walls, bridges, churches and take cruises along the Mediterranean. Like this book, these achievements, however minimal or magnificent, are simply the result of an unexpected surplus of leisure time – leaving us to balance a number of evolutionary paradoxes. Now, when we are not building edifices to ourselves, we use our surplus time to *discover* the meaning of life and tend to our *self-esteem*. In those thousands of years, we have turned away from our fundamental purpose. We now value *independence* over our association with others; *self-sufficiency* over partnerships; *self-indulgence* over collaboration, *distance* over proximity, *self-esteem* over self- and other-acceptance, *baby-mommas* over more child-friendly child-rearing and Internet porn over intimate relationships.

We continue to protect and reproduce, but we do it from a distance.

We form more satisfying intimate relationships over the airways.

We view aloofness, separation and exclusivity as signs of success.

We compete, rather than pool resources.

We reject criticism with anger and violence.

We set out to *out-do* one another.

We inflict misery on others and revel in our power to do so.

We have disguised our emotional connection to each other, because we have somehow begun to view our connection with others as a weakness:

If I show you respect, I am fragile.

If I am courteous toward you, I am inferior.
If I express dependence, I am weak.

It is my considered opinion that we are becoming a congested, angry and anxious community of people. We are growing by leaps and bounds. As a result, many of us have resorted to vulgarity, violence and disrespect.

I sometimes recognize this very thing in myself.

It may be that we are abandoning our most basic instinct to love and attach to members of our broader communities. We have forgotten how to connect, to care for one another and to cooperate. Just as it seems children have forgotten how to play outside, we may have just forgotten how to live together. We have become quite independent of others, to the exclusion of even knowing our neighbors. Many of us have lived in small neighborhoods or large cities for a major part of our lives and cannot name one neighbor or claim even one as a friend. We come and go, never connecting with others. We treat each other with such disregard, as if to do otherwise would be threatening, burdensome and oppressive.

We have lost common courtesy.

As we seek to improve our EI, we will attempt to once again make a purposeful connection with others, leading to a more satisfying emotional relationship with ourselves.

****

The bastardized concept of *self esteem* may have contributed to our contemporary social environment. It seems that people have somehow confused **courtesy, kindness, manners** and **politeness** with an expression of personal weakness and self deprecation. "If I am courteous to you, it means I am elevating you above myself. If I do that, I am somehow weakening my own value. We can't have that. I must never show deference or courtesy to anyone. To do so is to demean myself."

Every human experience that could once be met with manners and politeness seems to have become an emotional challenge, a tug-of-war over egalitarianism.

Who will yield first and show subordination?

It won't be me.

Who will win this struggle over self esteem?

I was in an ice cream shop with a friend last week. She told me about having ridden the bus every day for several months in the summer, watching as the sign in the ice cream shop window advertising **homemade peach ice cream** passed her by and then disappeared behind her. She didn't have a car, so she couldn't drive there on her own. To get off the bus meant she had to pay again to get back on.

I agreed to take her.

We both approached the ice cream *maiden* together. Of course, the woman stood behind the counter and stared at us as if she had no clue what we could possibly want.

Not a peep.

Just a blank stare at something on the wall behind me.

She did not greet us and she certainly didn't show any sign that she was glad to have our business. I said, "I will have a small cup of chocolate, chocolate chip." She reached her scooper into the frozen chest and put a lump of brown speckled ice cream into a small cup. She handed it to me and I moved along in the line.

"Hello," my friend said to the ice cream server, smiling, apparently oblivious to the woman's disinterest in her as a customer,

"How are you? I will have a large cup of peach ice cream." The server didn't respond. She just handed my friend a cup of ice cream and my friend moved down the line to pay. "I didn't like that woman's behavior," I said, grabbing several napkins and a couple of spoons. I handed my friend her share.

"Yes, I didn't either. She was cold and unfriendly."

"But you greeted her. You said, 'Hi! How are you?' You didn't even flinch."

"I'm used to that. I just expect it. I prepare for it, even before I walk in a place."

"Well, I wouldn't accept it."

"You have to accept it, silly. You don't have to like it, but you do have to accept it. You don't have a lot of options. Besides, it's easier than demanding that people change their behavior. You can expect that people will act a fool no matter where you go. They just do. It's a fact of life. Don't take yourself so seriously. You just think you're too good to give in first. Eat your ice cream."

"I talk about this stuff with people all the time. When I get in a situation where I can actually use it, I sometimes don't do so well."

"I have waited months to have some of this ice cream. I am not going to get myself all worked up just because the woman behind the counter is unhappy. I'd rather she was friendlier. It would have made the experience a lot more enjoyable. But I can still be *hap-i-licious* when other people are not."

"What did you do instead of making yourself unhappy?"

"Well," she said, pulling her empty spoon from her mouth and pausing to think, "I looked at her and I imagined she was *emotionally handicapped.* I don't make myself angry with handicapped people. If you know that people can treat you rudely, you can prepare for it. You can tell yourself what you will do instead when it happens. Prepare for it, honey. That way you don't get taken by surprise and ruin your own day."

This story was not only meant to show the learner that there is ample opportunity to use the EI skills in your daily life, but that we are all challenged to do better, no matter who we are. ***Not succeeding at what we hope to do is not a sign of complete and utter failure.*** It can be an opportunity for learning, not only for me but for the ice cream maiden and anyone who might have come before or after us in search of ice cream. We all have an opportunity to contribute to each other's resolve. If I had ***thought twice***, and greeted the woman from the perspective I demanded from her, she might have learned something from me. I would have also avoided that lingering thought of anger I can still conjure up today, every time I see a sign for peach ice cream.

"Hello! Are you having a bad day today?"

"Not really."

"Well, I hope not. Look at all this great ice cream you get to scoop into all day."

"It's not so much fun."

"I'm glad you're here to scoop it for me."

"Thank you."

"You're welcome. I will have some chocolate, chocolate chip."

Nothing can better bring you peace than yourself.

"Anyone can be angry – that is easy. But to be angry with the right person, to the right degree, at the right time, for the right purpose, and in the right way this is not easy."

Ten – *The dangers of self-esteem*

Our contemporary concept of ***self esteem***, unlike the concept introduced in the mid 1960s by Morris Rosenberg and Nathaniel Branden, has lost its wished-for meaning and intent. This innovative idea called *self-esteem* was proposed to provide people with a more ***balanced*** method for assessing the ***positive*** and ***negative*** features of their personalities and skills. Rosenberg and Branden intended to help what appeared to them to be a human penchant for self deprecation – basing one's entire human value on an assessment of one's negative characteristics. Fundamentally, the concept of *self esteem* was a way of celebrating humanness – human strengths **AND** human weaknesses – making self-evaluation a more equitable process of self-judgment.

Before we proceed to the next step in our EI improvement, let's talk a little about the dangers of our contemporary definition of self esteem by examining its conflict with two essential EI concepts:

- ***Independence*** from judgments made by others, helping you rely more on your own judgment of yourself

- *Valuing self acceptance* over the concept of self esteem

The concept of self esteem has lost its fundamental meaning. Now, instead of a fair and equitable self evaluation, we encourage the notion that people should ***outright deny that they have any shortcomings, weaknesses*** and ***failures*** at all and, instead, elevate themselves to a level of ***perfect goodness***. To even suggest that someone possesses the slightest flaw in h/er personality, skill or character is construed as an all-out attack on that individual's personhood. This contemporary definition of self-esteem makes life quite burdensome for most of us.

Humans are inherently a combination of ***good*** and ***not-so-good characteristics***. Celebrating that fact is essential to improving your emotional intelligence. Making mistakes, succeeding, failing and overcoming adversity are all human potentials. Making errors, blunders, slip-ups, *faux pas* and oversights in judgment are all very much among the possibilities for human behavior. Some of us are skinny, some fat, some genius and some not.

We are a cornucopia of difference!

But none of us is perfect.

I am a firm believer in setting ***achievable goals***.

Being perfect is not an achievable goal.

We are all ***works in progress*** that can only be truly evaluated after death. "Talk all you want about my faults when I'm dead. In the meantime, forgive me."

No one can be deemed ***entirely bad – or good***.

If we are trained to emphasize only our goodness, and deny our weaknesses, we cannot ever be fully human. But, the present-day concept of self esteem denies that we have any knowledge of our weaknesses and **NEITHER SHOULD ANYONE ELSE**! Our perfect goodness, our most unique and enviable talents, our finest traits become the things we use to identify ourselves. Our weaknesses become the thing we will fight to the death to keep secret (or at least left unspoken).

"I have positive self esteem, honey! I am nothing but terrific!"

"I AM PERFECT AND I KNOW IT!"

"You can't tell me anything. I have positive self esteem, so nothing you can say will have any effect on me."

We might replace the concept of self-esteem with the concept of *self-* and *other-acceptance*. That way, when we make a mistake, or someone acts foolishly, we can *think twice* about it and learn not to condemn ourselves or others for possessing human weakness. We can instead *think twice* and forgive the choices people make and hope they will do the same when we make mistakes.

People seeking to improve their EI can achieve more success in that regard when they recognize *truth* and *reality*, even when truth and reality are wholly unwelcome or disagreeable.

You are a fallible human being.

Say that out loud!

You have good points and bad points. There is no reason why you should be the only person on earth who doesn't. Despite your flaws and weaknesses, you are no less worthy or unworthy of affection, esteem or forgiveness. The same goes for how you accept the reality of others. There is no reason why people have to be reduced to a complete state of shit-hood, simply because they treat you unfairly or disrespectfully or in some way you do not prefer. You and the people you encounter do not have to behave in any other way than the way you and others choose to behave. The fact that you or others fail at behaving optimally is not sufficient cause to reduce yourself or others to a condition of absolute worthlessness.

Unpleasantness is never awful and it is nearly always bearable.

You are a grand combination of strengths, weaknesses, assets and flaws. To deny that dimension of yourself is to deny the promise you possess for learning, changing and evolving.

Celebrate your weaknesses!

Look them square in the eye.

Ultimately you might make a weakness into a positive force in your personality.

First, you will have to see your weaknesses.

Nothing can better bring you peace than yourself.

"Nature gifts human beings with two essential emotional potentials – fear and attachment – from which radiate a magnitude of culture-based variations. Joy, anger, delight and despair are products not of Nature but of the imagination."

Eleven – *Emotional Memory*

All behavior serves a purpose.

Thought is a behavior.

Emotion is a product of thought and, therefore, emotion serves a purpose.

If a particular emotion stops serving a purpose, you will stop using it and it will go ***extinct***. If you use a specific emotion enough, anger for example, it will be the emotion you use to address specific you face in life.

What purpose, then, do *your* emotions serve?

As previously discussed, fundamentally, there are two ***essential*** emotions common to most mammals – ***attachment*** and *fear*. Most mammals are born with a drive to attach to one another and to respond to threats to their own safety, their offspring and to members of their own tribes (or herds). Humans, unlike cows or foxes, however, possess the ability to derive ***lesser emotions*** from attachment and fear. For example, joy, sadness, delight, hatred, glee, disgust, ecstasy and despair may be viewed as *derivatives* of attachment and fear. Essentially, humans have more emotional range (and imagination) than any other animals.

At birth, we are designed to pursue one ambition – ***survival***. Nature has determined the gifting each human being with an innate potential for *fear* and *attachment* is likely to further that ambition. We might be born to Mormons, Pigmies, blacks, whites, Asians, Christians, Hispanics or cannibals. It hardly matters. Instinctively we are prepared to survive in *any civilization* where humans are the dominant species. Over time, our initial ambition to survive becomes more expansive. Although our early focus is on survival (fear), we are also learning to *adapt* and *assimilate* by committing to memory the ***rules*** of ***cooperation, congregation*** and ***copulation*** (attachment).

The ***rules*** of ***cooperation, congregation*** and ***copulation*** are primarily learned and result in the framework of our ***emotional education***. For the most part, the ***customs, mores*** and ***values*** that help us socialize within the confines of our *particular* families and navigate the interiors of our *broader cultures* are the primary factors that influence emotional learning and memory. Where one person, for example, may express *joy* and *delight* over a particular event, another person may respond just the opposite. Emotional memory is ***subjective*** and ***dependent on experience*** to cultivate.

Emotional memory is maintained by ***repeated use***.

If it is true that we ***learn*** from exposure to our culture how and when to emote (to express emotion) in order to obtain some ***desired result***, it would logically follow that emotion can be altered, in order to bring a different result. Altering emotion may rely on the following skills and acquired abilities:

- **Perceiving Emotions**: EI is often improved by recognizing that, in order to experience emotion, we must first *perceive* an event. ***An event by itself is benign*** but comes to emotional life through our perception of it.
- **Interpreting**: Following the perception of an event, we apply a skewed logic or internal language. That logic is dependent on experience and how true to the culture in which we were reared. Our unique internal language often includes the words ***should, ought, must, have to*** and ***need***.
- After applying this internal language, we promote a ***self-styled*** way of making sense of the event.
- **Application of Meaning**: An event can take on any number of *meanings*, depending on how it is perceived. The *meaning you apply to the event* will dictate your emotional response to it. The application of alternative meaning will, then, result in an alternative emotional response.
- **Function of Emotional Response**: The *function* of your emotional response (anger for example) is to *enforce the meaning* you apply to behavior. For example, if you interpret a behavior as *selfish*, the meaning you may apply could be: *People should not be selfish.* Your emotional goal (to express anger) is meant to cause others to view your *meaning* in the same way.
- **Managing Emotion**: In order to better manage your emotional response, you will first have to change the meaning you apply to an event. To do that, you will have to listen to your self-talk

– that voice in your head that says, *"People should not be selfish. People should behave differently. People should be more giving and selfless. I cannot stand it and I cannot live happily unless people behave better."*

- These pitfalls of emotional problem-solving can be addressed by ***thinking twice*** rather than perceiving once.

Nothing can better bring you peace than yourself.

*"If it is true that we **learn** from exposure to our culture how and when to emote (to express emotion) in order to obtain some **desired result**, it would logically follow that emotion can be altered, in order to bring a different result."*

Twelve – *Self Talk and Preparation*

We've discussed the *first* of *our strategies* that are likely to lead you to improved EI:

- **Committing** to change
- Using **articulated thought**
- **Identifying** the problem

And our insights:

- **Independence** from judgments made by others, helping you rely more on your own judgment of yourself
- **Valuing self acceptance** over the concept of self esteem

In Chapter Seven, we discovered that the *true* problem in our emotional adventure with the grocery store cashier was:

- "When I am treated disrespectfully, I tell myself *I shouldn't be* treated that way; I *need* respect from everyone I meet, and I *cannot stand it* when I don't get it."

We will continue to use this same problem with the cashier to complete the next part of the process:

- Promoting *emotional self-determination*
- Identifying *meaning*
- Begin by acknowledging that you are taking steps to *think twice*.
- Begin the process by promoting *emotional self-determination*
- Say out loud:
- "I am choosing to think twice."
- In this way, you are focusing your efforts on problem-solving, encouraging emotional self-determination and committing to change.
- In much the same way we set about finding the *true problem* by asking ourselves how the circumstance was a problem for us, finding *meaning* will lead you to an even higher awareness of the source of your problems.
- **Remember**: Your emotional issues are not normally related to any particular incident. They are more likely a result of how you *perceive* an incident and how you apply *meaning* to it.
- You will discover that not only is the problem yours to solve, but the solution will depend on your ability to find *meaning* in your own perception of the problem. The fact that the problem and its solution rest with you makes improved EI more of an achievable reality for you.
- After committing to thinking twice, ask yourself:
- "What does it *mean* to me that people treat me disrespectfully?

- What does it *mean* to me that I am not getting what I think I *need*?
- What does it *mean* to me to tell myself I *cannot stand it*?"
- Now answer your own questions:
- "When I am treated disrespectfully *it means* I am not being respected.
- "If I am not being respected, *it means* I am not respectable."
- "If I am not respectable, *it means* I am not likeable."
- "If I am not likeable, *it means* I am a bad person."
- "If I am a bad person, *it means* I am not a good person."

If you are going to make any kind of measurable progress in improving your EI, it will be essential to *first identify the problem* and *second,* identify what the issue *means to you*. The idea that people treat you unfortunately is only meaningful if you place some level of significance on it – and make some sort of *inference* about it. The person or people or place or circumstance you've encountered isn't likely to change simply because you *will* it to change. The *meaning* you apply to any circumstance, however, can always change. You have, over time, embedded meaning into your reasoning of any given situation. Identifying and committing to giving an event more *rational, self-enhancing* and *beneficial meaning* will be your challenge.

For more information on *identifying meaning*, see the section of this book marked *Sample Session*.

Nothing can better bring you peace than yourself.

"Remember, a situation unto itself is meaningless. For it to have meaning, you have to apply meaning to it."

Thirteen – *Emotion begins as thought*

There is a lot of discussion these days (at least in my little corner of the world) about latent and learned personality characteristics.

Is personality something that is learned?

Are our personalities a product of genetics and experience?

Or are our genetics the mortar that cements our personalities in place, even before our birth?

We should not be so ready to accept any theory of personality as a precise, unalterable explanation of who we are or who are children are likely to become. We might first ask ourselves what benefit we get from searching for a theory of personality to explain our behavior. "My quick temper is just a personality trait I inherited. We all act that way. There's nothing I can do about it;" or "According to the Myers-Briggs, I am an ISTJ. You are an ENFP. I thought you would be an INTJ and I would be an INFP. Who knew?"

Like hair color, blood type, eye color and skin color, we may actually inherit some features of our personality from our ancestors.

Why?

Well, our ancestors survived using a combination of skill and a number of adaptive personality characteristics. Our forefa/mothers were quite successful, essentially, at cooperating, congregating and copulating. Why not pass along those proven skills, the very thing that made all that happen? Our genetic promise *just may* surface as a familiar family trait.

"He's just like his father. They are both so private;"

"She and her mother are so analytical;"

"They both are so friendly; just like their cousins;"

"He and his grandmother are like twins. They have the very same sense of humor."

If your family members are known for their outgoing personalities, or their penchant for being disagreeable, under a wide variety of circumstances, you and your children could inherit a predisposition for those same characteristic in the expression of your own personalities. Of course, your ease at speaking in public or your skill at selling used cars may well be a result of simply living with people who are at ease speaking to groups or comfortable exaggerating the truth. You may have *learned* your behavior from your grandmother, rather than inherited it genetically from her. As well, you may have learned the behavior, but inherited a genetic potential for learning it.

This is getting confusing.

Here is what I'm getting at.

I once worked with a father who believed that his daughter inherited her penchant for lying from her mother.

"People can inherit personality characteristics you know! Her mother lied her ass off. She lied about everything. One lie after another. It was like she didn't even know what the truth was. My ex's mother used to lie like a rug, too. Neither one of them ever told me the truth about anything. It's an inherited thing. I'm sure of it."

"Do you think there might be something in your daughter's environment that may be inducing her to lie?"

"Well, her mother has been gone since she was two years old. It isn't anything I've done. I raise her to tell the truth. She's hard-wired that way."

"How do you want to attempt to help your daughter make better choices?"

"I guess we can't. It's in her genes. She's just like her mother and there's no way around that. She'll grow up to lie to her husband some day, too, I guess."

It's very hard to prove how much of personality is inherited (if it is at all) on a molecular level. (Twin studies make quite interesting reading, however.) Often, when it comes to personality development, generally, and human psychology, specifically, observation and guessing are, at times, all we have to go on. In truth, it hardly matters where your personality comes from, be it through inheritance or experience or a combination of both. It matters more to believe that your personality is under your control and can be adjusted, changed and repaired depending on your desire to do so. The wonder of your personality is its flexibility and adaptability to change. Improvement in emotional intelligence depends on that being our shared understanding.

****

I once had a learner who wanted to discuss her *eating disorder*. She too believed she inherited it from her mother – like her sister. "We all have eating disorders," she said. "We are all *wired* that way."

Professionally, I am a hard sell on nearly any psychological diagnosis. Diagnosis, I believe, replaces our unique human character with some clinical, cookie-cutter identity. That philosophy is often identified in how people describe themselves and others in terms of their clinical labels.

"I am **A MANIC-DEPRESSIVE**;"

"He **IS A** schizophrenic;"

"She **IS** A borderline personality;"

"He **IS** ADHD;"

"She **IS** Down syndrome."

As if these *poor incapacitated* and *forever-ill* people are the illustrations, **TEXTBOOK EXAMPLES,** of the conditions they are supposed to **BE**.

In fact, rather than **BEING** a mental health condition, people **HAVE** mental health conditions.

No one is the *epitome* – the walking example of a diagnosed mental health condition. In reality, diagnoses sometimes serve the purpose of giving *meaning* to people who, otherwise, view themselves as meaningless. Providing someone with a psychological or physical diagnosis (the more unique the better), can be the frame of reference from which people begin to understand themselves and their potential for growth and change.

I cannot imagine why anyone would tell a child s/he **IS** ADHD. ADHD will, from that moment on, become the frame of reference from which that child views every one of h/er failures and challenges for the rest of h/er life.

Nut heads!

As you might surmise from reviewing the first EI improvement steps outlined in this book, my learner with the eating disorder wasn't such a hard sell on diagnoses. She was convinced along with her eating disorder she also had ***obsessive compulsive disorder*** and ***a germ phobia***. The day I met with her, she was focused more on her ***eating disorder*** and ***needed*** help with better ***understanding*** her problems. (I find that people are often more interested in ***understanding*** their condition, rather than actively ***doing something about it***.) The following is an example of how we accomplished that goal:

EI Guide: *How can I help you?*

Learner: *After I eat, I put my fist in my mouth and make myself throw up.*

EI Guide: *How is that a problem for you?*

Learner: *I don't know; you tell me.*

EI Guide: *I will take a wild guess and say that you value yourself primarily on how thin you are?*

Learner: *You are right. But that doesn't help me* **understand** *why I make myself throw up.*

EI Guide: *What would it mean if you were heavier? More weighty?*

Learner: *It would mean that I was ugly and I wouldn't have any friends. It would mean my husband would divorce me. It would mean other women would criticize me."*

EI Guide: *It isn't likely that you wouldn't have any friends if you were weightier, unless you chose that outcome. Lots of weighty people have friends. I'll play along, though. What would it mean if you didn't have any friends?*

Learner: *It would mean that people didn't like me.*

EI Guide: *For those reasons, alone?*

Learner: *Yeah, I'm a* **good person***, otherwise.*

EI Guide: *Why don't we spend some time talking about the system you use to evaluate your worth, rather than why you stick your fist in your mouth? I can't stop you from doing that. That is something you will have to resolve to do. I can help you manage this idea that your bathroom scale and other people's opinions of you have become the source of your self-acceptance. Maybe once you take control of how you place value on yourself, you might find that you don't want to stick your fist in your mouth anymore.*

***

How on earth are we born with so much prospective for emotional achievement, yet we wind up *making ourselves throw up, murdering people who don't cooperate with us, punching people in the throat who speak their mind* and making ourselves *depressed when we find ourselves cheated on, taken advantage of, lied to* and *criticized?* (Remember we talked about how most emotion is a by-product of fear and attachment? Well, the answer to this question, for me, is to ask myself **what people are afraid of**. Once I discover the answer to that question, I can often begin to discover the source of nearly any emotional response I encounter in myself and others, e.g., "My partner doesn't love me anymore. What am I afraid of? I am afraid I will be alone. I am afraid I won't ever find anyone to love me again if he doesn't love me anymore. I am afraid I will be inconvenienced, uncomfortable, worried, scared and depressed and I won't be able to stand that. I'm afraid that I will be thought of as completely bad and unattractive because my partner rejected me."

That is a lot to be afraid of.

In an attempt ***not*** to continually burden my learner with brain anatomy, suffice it to say that your ***emotions begin as thoughts***, but can be viewed more microscopically as actual *physical substances – neurons, brain cells, little bubbles of knowledge* that hold the memories of your experiences. Here's another example of ***defining the problem*** and ***finding meaning***:

EI Guide: *So what happened?*

Learner: *She stared at me the wrong way. I could tell she was thinking,* You disgust me.

EI Guide: *Goodness, what did you do?*

Learner: *I told her to watch her face or I'd watch it for her.*

EI Guide: *How did you know she was thinking that particular thought about you? Maybe she ate something that upset her stomach.*

Learner: *Believe me; I've seen that face before. I know ridicule when I see it.*

EI Guide: *I'll play along. What was she doing, exactly?*

Learner: *Well, I was eating my baked cod and she was looking over at me.*

EI Guide: *How was that a problem for you?*

Learner: *She should be looking at her own plate. She shouldn't be staring at me. I need to have some privacy when I'm eating. You know what I mean?*

EI Guide: *I'm sure I don't. But let's just ask what this means, this looking and staring. What does it mean to you that she was doing all these things?*

Learner: *It means she was looking down at me because of the way I was dressed. I was wearing jeans and a tube top. This is America. A man can wear jeans and a tube top if he wants!"*

EI Guide: *Exactly. But what does it mean to you that she was looking at you that way?"*

Learner: *It means she thought I was foolish and a joke and that she was better than me."*

EI Guide: *And what would that mean?*

Learner: *That she was right?*

****

Through **repeated experience**, brain cells connect with one another and strengthen their bonds, forming *nuclei – clusters, collections, bubbles of knowledge*, like *balloons* in a bunch that have come together in an agreement to cooperate in order to achieve a future behavioral goal. *"If I see this kind of facial expression again, it means the person is thinking these thoughts. If people think these thoughts about me, then I cannot stand it."*

****

Let's imagine the interior of your skull at birth, before time and experience have had a chance to influence its development. Imagine that instead of white and gray brain matter we have a number of *partially-inflated*, very tiny balloons as a substitute. Few if any of the balloons are inflated to any real measure. Sort of like the week-old mass of balloons you gave your officemate for her birthday. They hover, barely afloat, limp and lifeless in the corner of her office.

Now, move that image to the interior of your skull and multiply it by *one hundred billion*. The human infant, whose only goal in life is to survive, explore and learn, begins to inflate and deflate those balloons through **experience** and **knowledge**. *"Mommy comes when I cry. Mommy feeds me when I'm hungry. Mommy holds me before I sleep. Mommy changes me when I poop. Mommy tells me I'm a good* boy." These experiences will inflate the balloons, forming what might eventually become the cluster dedicated to expressing emotional **trust**. *"Mommy doesn't come when I cry. Mommy doesn't feed me when I'm hungry. Mommy doesn't hold me before I sleep. Mommy doesn't change me when I poop. Mommy tells me I'm a good girl, but sometimes she tells me I'm a bad girl."* These experiences will form what might eventually become the cluster dedicated to expressing emotional **distrust**.

Regardless, with each passing day, the infant accumulates knowledge of the world *s/he lives in* and inflates h/er balloons with it. We can imagine that the infant is learning that people can, generally, be trusted or distrusted, depending on their early experiences and how they learned to inflate that cluster of balloons. We might call this cluster the ***trust/mistrust cluster (nuclei)***. We can use it to determine how the infant encounters others later in life.

EI Guide: *How can I help you?*

Learner: *I just can't trust my girlfriend.*

EI Guide: *How is that a problem for you?*

Learner: *Well, she says she is going to visit her sister, but something tells me she isn't really going there. I think she is lying to me.*

EI Guide: *What sort of things do you suspect she is doing?*

Learner: *Cheating?*

EI Guide: *Is there some reason to believe that?*

Learner: *Not really. She is very nice to me.*

EI Guide: *Then what are you telling yourself in the face of this contradictory information?*

Learner: *I guess I tell myself that the people I love just can't be trusted. They will forever let you down.*

EI Guide: *We have some work to do.*

As a child matures, many hundreds of thousands of other experiences are also working to fill the remaining 99.99 billion other balloons, simultaneously. The child may be learning such social customs as, *What can I expect on my birthday? When can I expect and receive affection? What do I do when I meet strangers? How, when and what do I eat? What happens when I make a mistake? How do I feel about myself? How is affection expressed? When am I a bad boy/girl? How can I become good again? How am I punished when I fail? Where do my emotions come from? What must happen in order for me to feel content again?*

The answers to each of these questions are stored in the balloons, eventually resulting in a skull filled brightly colored, inflated spheres. The balloons and their content become the rules by which you engage others. Through repeated experience, you keep them afloat. Give the balloons air (a mixture of knowledge and experience), and they will rise and become strong and powerful sources of information. Leave them alone, and they will eventually deflate to the point where they will fall away, lay flat on the floor of your skull, go to sleep, yet capable of inflating at some point in the future when they are needed.

I was speaking with a colleague about this particular analogy. "You've really simplified the process," she said. "Can you give me some kind of real-life experience I can draw on to remember the lesson?"

"Let's say your own child was whisked away from you at birth. And let's say he was handed over to a family in Turkey. Do you think your child would be someone you would later recognize?"

"I'd recognize him," she said, "He's blond and blue-eyed."

"His language, behavior, his customs, his values, even his religion would be very different from your own, though. Those balloons would be filled with the knowledge of Turkish customs and traditions."

"I can't imagine that he wouldn't be Christian."

"Imagine it. He could be Christian. It is more likely though that he would be Muslim – probably Sunni."

"That's worth thinking about."

"Let's say you got him back when he was twelve. What would you have to do to assimilate him into your family and your customs and traditions?"

"Using your analogy, I guess I would have to find a way to deflate those balloons and fill them up with different information."

"Do you imagine it would be easy to change the way he thinks?"

"No! Not easy at all. I'm not even sure how I would do that. Maybe I would just get a pin and start popping."

"If thinking, perceiving and behavior change were as easy as simply popping balloons, I would be writing books on how to sharpen pins. It will be very difficult for you to change the way you respond to the others when you set a goal to think twice. It will take a lot of work, dedication, time and hope."

Changing the structure of your brain takes determination, dexterity, dedication and skill. It takes practice and mental agility.

Something more in line with learning the very skilled sport of darts, rather than randomly popping balloons.

Now there's a parallel for another time.

Nothing can better bring you peace than yourself.

"Our quest to establish the rules of our behavior, however, frequently does not extend much further than our immediate families and our neighborhoods."

Fourteen – *Think Twice*

Before we go on to the final step in the **Think Twice** EI paradigm, I want to emphasize the importance of the ***imaginary balloons*** we talked about earlier and review the previous steps.

Balloons (or neurons, brain cells, gray matter) contain *knowledge*. *Knowledge* derived from experience is the substance that inflates the balloons and can be better defined as your *beliefs*. *Beliefs* are your certainties, the psychological state in which you hold a premise to be true. It is not likely that any of your *beliefs* can be proved through anything except your willingness to agree to and give force to them.

You acquire your *personal truths* and pack those truths into those balloons through experience within a number of distinct settings. First, you are reared in a particular home – a home that teaches you a majority of the truths you now hold. You practice and test these truths in school, in social settings within your own community and, eventually, in your career and your own family. You teach these beliefs to your children. What are your personal truths? Which of your personal truths would benefit from a comprehensive review?

My Partial List of Self-Defeating Truths

"It is true that if I make a mistake, I am bad."

"It is true that I can only be good when someone tells me I am good."

"It is true that I make people angry and they, in turn, make me angry."

"It is true that I make people miserable and vice versa."

"It is true that if I make a mistake, I am an utter failure."

"It is true that I can break someone's heart."

"It is true that I embarrass myself and others."

"It is true that I make people cry."

"It is true that that if I behave according to the rules, without error, I can expect to be treated well and be viewed as a good person."

Now that my personal truths are on display for the world to see, I would encourage you to make a list of your own personal truth.

Your early *emotional education* is the means by which you have become dependent on others for your personal value, state of mind, ability to determine your own successes and weaknesses and the authority to seek your own approval or disapproval of your own behavior. A partial list of your own self-defeating truths, the truths you hold about yourself that influence your emotional life and your improved emotional intelligence would be a grand start toward improving your emotional intelligence.

****

Let's review the first few steps of our *Think Twice* EI paradigm, before we talk about the final step:

- **Reflection**
- Emotional *Evolution*

In order to complete the EI articulated thought paradigm, we will continue with our imaginary experience with the cashier at the grocery store. (My learner will be, after reading this book, at minimum, quite adept at experiencing poor customer service in a grocery store.)

❖ In *Step One*, we focused on *articulating thought.*

- We articulated thought and answered the question, *"What happened?"*
- *What did I see?*
- *What did I hear?*
- *What was said?*
- *Is this information true? Verifiable?*
- Remember, you are articulating your own thoughts. You are being detailed, but only articulating the facts. Your goal is not to embellish, exaggerate or provide details that didn't really occur. Unlike this example:
- "So I'm like shut up, and she's like no way you just up, and I'm like no you shut up, and she's like you look like my ass, and I'm all like I didn't know I was that fat, and she's like you shut up and I'm like you shut up, and she's like no way you shut up, and then she's all like all uppity and I'm like shut up."
- Your articulated thought should leave no room for assumption, supposition or guessing. If it didn't actually happen, don't

speculate. Don't be tempted to tell yourself what you *knew* the cashier was thinking or feeling – unless she came out and told you. Don't be tempted to add detail that isn't there. *Just the facts*.

- Once we are clear on the facts, we must then ask ourselves, *"How is this situation a problem for me?"*
- After all, there was nothing inherently upsetting about the cashier's behavior to begin with, except that *you didn't like it* and you *applied meaning* to it.
- The fact is everyone experiences the cashier differently. My sister, for example, wouldn't even have remembered talking to the cashier. She would have driven home singing to the radio. Get her on the phone with a cable representative who wants to tell her over the phone how to set up her own Kindle and you will see a significantly different response.

❖ *Step Two*: So, how was it a problem for you?

- Your responses may include:
- "It was a problem for me because I didn't like it."
- "It was a problem for me because she shouldn't behave that way to customers."
- "It was a problem for me because I cannot stand it."
- "It is a problem for me because I need respect from the people I meet and talk with."
- "It is a problem for me it shouldn't happen. People should treat me better. I need respect to feel good about myself. I must have respect at all times so I can be happy. People have to do as I wish, or else.

- You will be keen to address the *self-defeating conclusions* you make from your experiences.
- In *Step Three* you searched for *meaning* in your problem statement.
- You asked yourself:
- "What does it *mean* to me if I am treated disrespectfully?"
- You may have answered:
- "It means I am not worthy of respect."
- "It means I view myself as *entirely good* except when I am treated badly. Then I view myself as *entirely bad*."
- The inference you draw from the experience is up to you to complete. Your answer to what *anything* means is the very thing that creates your emotional response to it.

****

Our final step is a process of establishing a framework for reflecting on the conclusions we drew from our *meaning statements*, finding *truth* and *untruth* in these statements and formulating *better meaning statements*.

- ❖ *Step Four* provides you with the opportunity to *challenge the meaning you apply to the situation*. At this point you will confront the inferences you draw from your experience.
    - You will ask yourself to provide legitimacy to the claim that you *NEED* the respect, regard, esteem, affection or honor of others in order to live *hap-i-licious-ly* in your life.
    - Is it true that I need respect from this person to be content with myself?

- Is it true that I *need* to be treated respectfully?
- Is it true that you *cannot stand it* when you are treated disrespectfully or is it that you simply *don't like it*?
- You will ask yourself to *confirm* the idea that anyone *should, ought, must or has to* behave better toward you than they choose to behave.
- Should people behave by my rules or do they make their own rules?
- Can I live with the idea that I don't control everyone's behavior?
- You will ask yourself to *corroborate* the suggestion that if someone behaves toward you in a way you don't like that it is somehow connected to your worth as a human being.
- If people make obvious poor choices with their behavior, does that make them entirely bad?
- If I make a mistake in my behavior, does that make me entirely bad, rotten and valueless?
- You will ask yourself where your *inspiration* comes from to make yourself unhappy, simply because someone else chooses to behave poorly.
- Is your response part of your fight, flight or freeze response? Is your body responding to threat?
- You may find, after reflecting on your self-talk that there really never is any real evidence that people *should, ought, must, have to or need* to behave any better toward you than they behave toward anyone else.

- People do not have to recognize your power, your social position, your money, your status, your age, your sex, or any other aspect of you that you hold so dear.
- People can ignore your imagines self image, celebrate it or criticize it.
- If you place your worth in the hands of others, it will always be, well, in the hands of others.
- People don't NEED TO BEHAVE DIFFERENTLY. YOU NEED IT! And if you want to get better, you are going to have to learn to NEED IT LESS.
- Logically, after you have this *reflection discussion* with yourself, you will conclude that being treated rudely, disrespectfully, uncaringly, insolently, discourteously or impolitely is not horrible, awful, unbearable, or that you cannot stand it.
- Of course being treated according to some acceptable civil standard is preferred, but it is not essential to your happiness.
- Although being treated noxiously is an unfortunate experience, it is **NOT** sufficient to cause alarm.
- If someone doesn't like you or when you think you are being treated badly or disrespectfully those circumstances are not sufficient to cause for alarm.
- The **ONLY** sufficient cause for alarm is the *meaning* you place on the event.

****

In order to evolve your less-manageable first thought to one that is more manageable, you will have to be willing to build a more expansive emotional imagination. Your success at using more accurate, self-enhancing meaning statements (self-talk) will be a tough slog; this milestone, however difficult, may provide you with a stronger foundation for achieving emotional evolution.

Your first thought when facing adversity (if unmanageable) is often an irrational assumption, primarily used as a protective device. Your second thought, if better constructed than your first, will provide you a way back to **emotional balance**. Remember, your narrow, linear thinking (first thought) is what got you into your emotional muddle in the first place. Your second thought, if deliberately refashioned, will bring you out of it.

When you think twice, you can begin to broaden your emotional possibilities, opening up a world of alternative choices.

You can imagine any number of less threatening scenarios than the one you imagine you are facing. For example, you can suppose that the person who is behaving disrespectfully toward you is emotionally handicapped and, therefore, more deserving of patience and care than anger and rage. Changing your perspective, using your imaginative potential, may help with evolving your unmanageable emotion to one that is less self-defeating.

Your emotional imagination is limitless.

You will have to think twice, however, to give your emotional imagination more breadth and width.

Your emotional evolution will depend on replacing the feelings you normally use with those that are more likely to bring better emotional and physical results – an emotion that is less random, more focused and self-determined.

We all want to evolve from anger to happiness – as soon as possible. That ideal, as we discussed, isn't likely to be achieved without establishing a new personal definition of happiness, a derivative of facts not conjecture, using your expansive imagination.

So what is left?

There are many emotions that could reasonably replace anger and bring about a more self-enhancing emotional state. What you replace anger with will be entirely your own choice. For instance, forgiveness, sadness, contentment, calm, peace and serenity are likely to be more manageable than anger and rage. These emotions are all, for me, very reasonable options, as well. The key factor to consider when deciding which emotion you will use to replace your anger or rage is to choose something you can willingly accept as a replacement. For example, a person who hopes to quit smoking by replacing cigarettes with eating broccoli may be choosing an insufficient substitute for smoking. Broccoli may not provide the smoker with good results. If forgiveness is NOT something you can reasonably use as a suitable replacement for your anger, don't set that emotion as your emotional goal. If you can't find an emotion you would rather express than anger, you may simply have to accept incremental change. You may reasonably evolve your emotion from anger x 9 to angry x 3. That, my learned friend, is the definition of emotional evolution.

You can try to do better next time. For now, you will have to learn to evolve your emotion to something less self-defeating and more manageable by learning to think twice.

Nothing can better bring you happiness than yourself.

****

As we discussed in previous chapters, it is best to develop a ***personal definition of happiness*** that includes such things as ***let down*** and ***disappointment***. "My definition of happiness includes the fact that I am sometimes visited by unfortunate events in my life. I can accept that and I can be content, even when things don't go my way."

Holding a ***strict*** definition of happiness is likely to result in long periods of unhappiness – unless the definition includes the realities of life. Without a broader definition of happiness, any disruption to your strict meaning may result in your sudden decent into despair.

Knowing you control your own definition of ***happiness*** and contentment will give you the leeway you need to step away from your traditional response and allow you to express any number of emotions to various stimuli. I, personally, try to express some level of ***forgiveness*** for people who make poor emotional choices. This is the emotion that works best for me. I have to admit that it gets a little bit easier the more I do it.

Don't expect everything to change overnight.

This EI paradigm takes practice, practice and more practice. Whatever amount of practice you put into it will bring you more benefit than you get now, thinking only once.

You will have to learn to ***think twice***.

Write out your more-reasonable definition of happiness and read it out loud.

Nothing can better bring you peace than yourself.

*"Through **repeated experience**, brain cells connect with one another and strengthen their bonds, forming nuclei – clusters, collections, bubbles of knowledge, like balloons in a bunch that have come together in an agreement to cooperate in order to achieve a future behavioral goal."*

Fifteen – *I wasn't raised like that!*

Is it possible to distinguish humans from the complex influence of their biological brain functions and their intricate social behaviors?

Yes!

And it is that human potential that we depend upon to achieve improved EI. Essentially, we are wired for social learning and we will assimilate to any environment we enter – if we choose to. We are **NOT**, however, wired for any *particular* type of social learning. One culture is as good as any other, apparently, as long as it includes ***cooperation, congregation*** and ***copulation***. We are wired to adapt to cultures that include these concepts. We are primarily social creatures, wired to express personality and to connect with others. We may even have an innate urge, a drive, to learn and to become ***expert at how to behave in groups***. We are not likely to survive in cultures that ignore these essential human activities. It appears that, without contact with others, we would wither.

"I've never been around those people. What should I do?"

"Just be yourself"

"Which self? The one who farts, watches television in his underwear and swears?"

"On second thought, follow my lead. Pretend you don't know me. We don't want to offend anyone. You have something on your lip."

Once we learn and practice what we have determined to be the limits of our own social behavior, significant effort is frequently put into ensuring everyone else follows the rules, too.

You should . . .

You ought . . .

You must . . .

You have to . . .

You need . . .

And we tend to the rules, like neat rows of champion budding tulip bulbs, ensuring that they are passed on to generations without modification.

We have a *Constitution*.

We have *Ten Commandments*.

We have family *rules*.

We have *laws*.

We have *punishments, consequences* and *outcomes*.

We do all of this, ostensibly, to increase our numbers and to survive as a species into the next millennia. The practice of establishing custom and convention *may* be innate in humans. The rules, themselves, however, may be *quite arbitrary and unique to human imagination*.

****

Scientists have traced human social behavior back over 40,000 years, concluding, to a large extent, that social learning and its corresponding behavior serve an adaptive purpose, integral to the continued existence of our species. Researchers from varying disciplines have observed that, in many ways, human evolution has not significantly sacrificed primitive social custom. We are still very much motivated to congregate, cooperate and copulate.

It seems we have more time on our hands, however, than our primitive ancestors ever dreamed of.

Like our long-ago relatives, we remain focused on seeking and receiving affection, albeit in varying and progressive ways. In fact, we don't actually have to physically meet other people anymore. To have a fulfilling relationship, we just have to have an active Internet connection and an attractive, youthful and very trendy avatar.

Likewise, we have never had more opportunity to congregate with other cultures than we do today. When our cell phone goes berserk or we lose our Internet connection, for instance, we find ourselves, like magic, suddenly speaking with a stranger in India or the Philippines, working together to resolve our problems, often while speaking different languages.

And we continue to respond to threats to our safety, only now we kill over such things as disrespect, assaults to our egos and our treasured self-esteem.

We are creatures of evolutionary custom, tradition and consequences, all of which appear to be inextricably blended to form our ever-advancing emotional wisdom.

"You shouldn't treat me like that!"

"How am I treating you?"

"You are ignoring me."

"I'm eating."

"You can eat and talk to me at the same time."

"I wasn't raised like that."

"You hate me!"

We are truly a world of nut-heads.

****

Social custom varies from home to home, culture to culture, place to place. In my home, it was considered taboo to put cigarette ashes on a plate where food had once been served. No one in my family would even think of spitting into a sink. My sister and her husband think it is considered bad form not to tip a waitress at least 25%, even if the service was horrid. I have witnessed on a few occasions where a family will say *Grace* **after** eating.

Why?

Blessing food before eating may lead to throwing away *blessed* food, if it is not all eaten. Walking through a cranberry bog in the fall is (cough) a mortal sin. Talking about one's successes is considered **gauche**, even if someone asks what you have been up to for the past five years. I have found it is best to hide one's accomplishments and pretend to be as miserable as the person asking.

There are a number of consequences for violations of these and other customs and traditions, ranging from ridicule to ostracization and shunning. Our quest to establish the rules of our behavior, however, frequently does not extend much further than our immediate families and our neighborhoods. Of course, some of our established rules of engagement extend well beyond the boundaries of our neighborhoods, communities and states. Some of our rules and customs are prevalent in all world cultures.

Regardless of how common they are, the rules we live by are **subjective**. There is nothing natural about respect, honesty, criticism or self-esteem. What is natural is *fear* and **attachment**. The derivatives of these emotions and their subsequent behaviors are each a product of group living

What may be viewed as *improper* in one culture may meet *acceptance* in another. The same behavior may result in taking your life in your hands. For example, men and women in Western cultures expect to be offered a hand when meeting new people and would be *offended* if that were not to happen. (Our culture has even begun to offer a hug as an initial greeting.) While shaking hands (or hugging) is viewed as an expected pleasantry by Westerners, Eastern cultures may be *shocked* at the forwardness of strangers reaching for them in such a familiar way – preferring, instead, to bow as a sign of respect – saving such intimate contact for very few others. Hand gestures are a common method of communication in almost all world cultures. Hand gestures, however, are habitually misinterpreted.

Custom often varies in how a certain culture may view traditional marriage, marriage between near-blood relations, marriage between same-sex partners, courtship, hospitality, etiquette, funerals, burials, polygamy, adultery and public displays of affection. In 1999 an Afghani living in Maine was arrested for kissing his infant son's genitals (a traditional Afghani expression of affection). Cambodian parents place hot objects on their children's foreheads during an illness. Cultures vary in the way they treat men and women, children and adults. We often assimilate to all of our familial, community and cultural learning. And we make the grand leap of assumption that everyone else should too.

Because it's right!

South Africa is a multicultural society, expressing many different customs, by and large influenced by indigenous African, English and Dutch custom. A close friend of mine, a missionary, visited South Africa several years ago and returned to his home state of Vermont with his new Zulu bride.

As you may imagine, Zulu culture consists of a number of atypical customs not known to the average Vermonter. For example, a man's wealth is measured in livestock.

My friend had two dogs and a ferret.

Very poor, indeed.

When a man wishes to marry a Zulu woman, he gets permission from the woman's father. After being granted the privilege, the two men agree on the payment of a *lebola* (a predetermined number of cattle). Once married, the woman is expected to wear a particular color of beads around the hem of her skirt and in her hair. This is a sign for all, much like our western wedding ring, that the woman is married and worthy of an elevated place in the social structure.

Despite the migration of many Zulu to larger cities, customs continue to influence their behavior. Throughout his courtship my friend was informed by his betrothed that permission to marry was granted by the woman's father. The price of a *lebola* should be arranged and paid at the time the request is made. My friend discounted these demands stating, "I'm not doing that. It's old fashioned and foolish. I don't have any cattle, besides."

"It would be a ***gesture***. That's all you need to do. Make a gesture. It would make everything more traditional. He likes tradition."

My friend's fiancé convinced him to invite her father and mother to dinner. "You can talk with him. Get permission to marry. Discuss the *lebola*. He's old fashioned. He would like that. He isn't really looking for payment. He would appreciate the gesture." Upon reaching the restaurant, my friend held the door for his guests, and they hesitantly entered the restaurant before him. That evening, there was no discussion of permission or *lebola*. On the way home, my friend's fiancé asked him why he hadn't discussed the issues of marriage. "It's all just foolishness," he said.

"It wouldn't have mattered anyway," she said. "They were very unhappy before they even sat down."

"Why?"

"In Zulu culture, the host is always supposed to enter a room *before* his guest."

"Americans don't do that. It considered rude."

"Of course; but it *is* our custom. You offended them."

"Really?"

My friend convinced his fiancé to marry him, without paying any tribute to custom and tradition. Her father would never recognize him as his son-in-law and distanced himself from his daughter. He and his new wife soon moved to Vermont, prepared to build a home together. But, instead of settling in comfortably, the weight of losing her family and contact with her father and the contrasts between Zulu culture and the people of Vermont were too much to bear. So much so that my friend's new wife began to show signs of mental instability. She talked a lot about the how she had no connection to the people she came from or the people around her. She couldn't tell right from wrong, good from bad, insult from admiration. The climate, the political, social and economic changes were too abrupt for her, sending her into a kind of emotional shock. Essentially, she had no idea how to behave with the members of her new community. After less than a year, she returned to South Africa, alone. My friend and his Zulu bride were soon divorced. My friend's Zulu wife, ostensibly, deflated all of her balloons at the same time, putting her into some level of emotional shock.

Improvement in your EI will depend on your increased dexterity to take control of these imaginary balloons and control how much or how little they are inflated and deflated.

Nothing can better bring you peace than yourself.

*"Your early **emotional education** is the means by which you have become emotionally dependent on others for your personal value, state of mind, ability to determine your own successes and weaknesses and the authority to seek your own approval or disapproval of your own behavior."*

Conclusion

I do want to briefly mention, before we part, that when you are ***in the moment*** of noxious emotional stimuli, you are not likely to make a lot of progress toward building or maintaining your emotional intelligence. The influence of your body's ***natural immediate reaction to frightening thoughts and perceptions*** and your focus on fighting, fleeing or freezing oftentimes overpowers your ability to embark on an organized and logical problem-solving adventure.

Truth be told, your body is too focused on protecting you from perceived harm to even allow for a change in the spotlight.

Experience your body's physiological response to misfortune. Learn the signs, the signals, the messages your body is sending. Feel the flush of blood to your face and neck. Sense your heart beating faster, those hormones surging through your bloodstream.

Breathe.

Learn to *take a very deep and satisfying breath* – not for the sake of taking deep breaths, but to stimulate the *vagus nerve*, an activity that will ultimately bring your body to a focused balance and a better likelihood of resolving your emotional issues.

While you wait for the chemicals your body is producing to dissipate, don't forget to forgive yourself for not responding the way you had planned and practiced.

Start over.

Think twice.

Again.

And again.

Remember, you are not likely thinking rationally when you think you are being chased by a polar bear. (You can learn to try.) Your body and mind respond to noxious human behavior in much the same way as it responds to a wild beast chasing you up a tree. And you are not likely, under either circumstance, to think rationally. Once you get free, and feel safe again, you can begin the process of thinking and planning how to make an effective weapon (new thoughts) if the same or a similar situation arises again.

Postponing your emotional improvement does not mean that you shouldn't commit to doing something about your perception of threat at some point after you have removed yourself from the threat. You may just have to learn to breathe and plan for when you can reasonably resolve the issue.

Simply said, your nutty thinking will almost always overpower your *rational thinking* – while in the moment. (You will spend at least as much time to *change your first thought* as it took to build it in the first place. So, if you are 37 years old, you can plan on *completing changing your first thought* in at least that amount of time. Until then, plan, practice and breathe.)

****

It may be important to distinguish between long-term and **episodic emotional stimuli.**

Episodic exposure is short-term and time-limited. Long-term emotional stimuli, however, is often characterized by complaints about one's job, the neighbors' dog, a boss, the neighbors, a son's new bride, the neighbor's kids, the mailman or the color of the neighbors' house. These issues are not expected to go away anytime soon, meaning that you may have to **commit every day** to improving your emotional intelligence in relation to the very same issues.

I have found that if you are experiencing long-term emotional issues, you are challenged not to resolve that particular issue, but to resolve how your damaging thoughts about the issue influence other dimensions of your life.

Long-term noxious stimulus appears to have a viral quality to it.

To truly begin to resolve long-term noxious thinking and behaving, you will be more successful at improving your emotional intelligence, once you remove yourself permanently from it, e.g., get a new job, move to another neighborhood or start picking up your mail at the post office. In the meantime, you will have to accommodate the long-term stimulus and learn to be committed to balancing your emotional life, in spite of it.

Living long-term with noxiously-behaving others is something like living in full view of a bucket of poisonous snakes. No matter how long you live next to them, you will likely experience, to some degree, fear and loathing in response to them. You do, however, still have to live your life and survive, in spite of them. You may never like living alongside a bucket of poisonous snakes, but, in time, you may learn to tolerate one another.

Along with a bucket of poisonous snakes, improving your emotional intelligence can be compared to losing weight. It seemed effortless to put the weight on. Before you knew it, you were tipping the scales at a weight you never imagined was possible for you. Setting a goal to lose the extra added pounds was easy. Overcoming ***procrastination*** and ***laziness***, however, proved to be an even bigger goal than actually losing the weight. It's a lot easier to eat the way you've grown accustomed. It seemed effortless to establish your ***nutty thinking***. It will seem, at times, almost hopeless to reshape it.

You may experience the same kind of laziness while seeking to improve your emotional intelligence.

This weight loss analogy is a proper reminder of how much effort you will have to dedicate to improving your emotional intelligence – and maintaining that improvement. You may fail; you may make some headway, and you may have to postpone your improvement. But like anything else you set your mind to, you will have to just keep trying.

****

And then there are the children.

If we, as a human species, are going to ***purposefully*** survive into the next millennia, we will have to begin by tending better to our children's emotional health.

My unscientific appraisal of our contemporary culture leads me to believe that we are becoming increasingly more congested, angry, fearful and anxious. It appears, if this is true, we must begin to contribute more positively to the emotional development of children. We cannot be content that once our children behave *exactly* like we do, we are finished with their social educations. Teaching children that their emotions come from some external source (from other people and things rather from their own thinking) is maladaptive, harmful and will likely result, later in life, in beating, bullying or coercing others into submission.

I would be *hap-i-licious* if children attended *Emotional Intelligence schools*, instead of kindergarten. After all, children have their whole lives to learn to read, write and recognize the similarity between the smell of hydrogen sulfide gas and a fart. Early childhood education may be better managed if it were to focus exclusively on teaching children how to behave more rationally and to get along better with *themselves* and others. Teach children how to cooperate, to be good leaders and followers. Teach them how to relate to customers, to manage their emotions, to stay motivated and to take initiative. That would be a better use of the time we devote to early childhood education.

And don't let up.

Make *emotional intelligence* an obligation of our system of education. We might identify measureable levels of social change using that topic as an educational benchmark – as opposed focusing exclusively on achieving higher test scores.

****

Your struggle to improve your EI will be in how consistent, focused and determined you can be in using the skills found in this book, forming new thoughts and behaviors and sharing your knowledge with children.

Children have very expansive and impressionable minds. It seems nearly anything we tell them becomes a point of fact from which they judge future experiences. Rather than learning to think twice, children can very well learn to ***think once and for all***, securing for themselves a less burdensome emotional future. If we continue to teach children to kill one another over such things as *disrespect,* gold jewelry and stereotypes – to wage war over religion and political dogma and to contribute to the suffering of others based on centuries of vendetta or imagined slight, we surely cannot evolve our human emotional potential to accommodate a future where our only expectation is more anxiety, anger and human congestion. We will be forever stuck, instead, with making sense of our world through the narrow scope of ***fear*** and ***attachment*** we were born with thousands of years ago, gauging our happiness against an unrealistic, perfect standard and responding to the slightest inconvenience as if it were a threat to our very existence.

****

Passing on the idea, from generation to generation, that our present method of emotional reasoning is somehow optimal will do nothing to help evolve our species. In fact, our current method of behaving and emoting is wholly maladaptive, ill-functioning and is, simply, a conked out idea. We have to learn to think and behave differently, more rationally and with more imagination. Of course, we cannot hand down this imaginative method of emoting to our children without first modeling rational behavior ourselves.

That is the tough part.

Frankly, I am very tired of being responsible for how other people make themselves feel all day. I am even more tired of having to settle on restricting my behavioral and emotive potential to the magical idea that I *make people feel* – simply to suit the people around me. I would prefer, instead, to say, "Own your own feelings and leave me out of it! I have my own feelings to own." But, as I emphasized in the beginning of this book, if we stand strong, shoulder to shoulder, and make this statement as the small group of emotionally intelligent folk, we will likely limit our opportunity to *cooperate, congregate* or *copulate* with the majority of people who simply will not hear of it.

So we carry on, compromising our sanity and the sanity of future generations by continuing with this magical idea that our feelings somehow come from how other people *make us feel*. Fully aware, however, that nothing can better bring us peace than ourselves.

Sample Sessions

Let's put a little *in vivo* (in life) experience behind what we have learned so far. I chose these particular learners because the issues are fraught with concerns about self-esteem and other disturbing cognitions.

EI Guide: How can I help you?

Learner: I have to clean. I am always cleaning. If there is a spot on the kitchen counters, I have to clean the cabinets out, wash the floor, clean out the refrigerator and wipe everything down with Clorox.

EI Guide: How is that a problem for you?

Learner: I don't understand. How is it a problem for me? I thought that was obvious.

EI Guide: It isn't. I am trying to understand your message. Can you tell me how this cleaning thing you do is a problem for you?

Learner: I guess when you put it that way it really isn't a problem for me. Actually, I like having a clean kitchen.

EI Guide: Wonderful. What would it mean if you had messy countertops and messy a messy refrigerator?

Learner: It would mean that I was a shitty housewife.

EI Guide: If you were a shitty housewife, what would that mean?

Learner: It would mean I was a shitty mother.

EI Guide: What would it mean if you were a shitty mother?

Learner: It would mean I was a shitty wife.

EI Guide: What would that mean?

Learner: That my husband would leave me.

EI Guide: And . . .

Learner: I would be alone.

EI Guide: With that much at stake, I can see now how you have placed so much emphasis on keeping your kitchen clean.

Learner: I don't like it, but I see where you're going now.

***

In the above dialogue, we have *perception* of an event: *Cleaning countertops, cabinets, floors and the refrigerator.* If the learner were helping herself, she would retell this event out loud to herself with as much detail as possible. Remember, telling the story out loud helps keep you focused on problem-solving.

Next, after being very clear about what happened, the learner will ask herself out loud, *"How is this a problem for me?"* In this case the learner stated, *"I guess when you put it that way it really isn't a problem for me. Actually, I like having a clean kitchen."*

Asked and answered.

The issue, however, holds some significance for the learner, so the follow-up questions is, *"What would it **mean** if you had messy countertops and messy a messy refrigerator?"* This question causes the learner to focus on her thinking, rather than the event itself. The learner then applies her own meaning to the event, drawing the conclusion that cleaning has some connection to her value as a mother, wife and individual person. Here is where the work in therapy begins.

EI Guide: Is it true that if you have a messy countertop that you are a failure as a mother, wife and human being? Is it true that you will live a worthless and unremarkable life if your kitchen floors are dirty?

Learner: Yes.

EI Guide: Prove it.

Learner: You're tough. I always thought I had OCD. I thought we were going to treat that condition.

EI Guide: I'm not sure what OCD is. I am sure that this is a real problem for you, so let's try to stay focused on the problem. Prove to me that you are irredeemable if you fail at keeping your kitchen clean.

Learner: Help me.

EI Guide: Well, simply, is it true that you have no value as a mother or a wife or a human being if your kitchen is dirty?

Learner: I think that, yes.

EI Guide: In that case, what do you think we have to do to get you to think differently?

Learner: OK.

EI Guide: Do you have any other redeeming qualities other than keeping your kitchen clean?

Learner: Yes, I organize a car pool. I am also an attorney, but I have taken time off for my kids. I clip coupons. I'm a pretty good cook. Yes, I have a number of redeeming qualities.

EI Guide: Then does it hold true that you are irredeemable when you kitchen is dirty?

Learner: I guess not; but I still don't like it.

EI Guide: Not liking it and reducing your value to nothing because of it are very different.

We *manage our emotion* by repeating to ourselves (through self talk) that something is true when it isn't and will not stand up to even the slightest scrutiny.

In order to manage emotion better, to increase our emotional intelligence, we have to confront the ***meaning*** we apply to the event.

And we have to learn to tell ourselves not only something different, but something that can stand the test of reason.

***

Let's use one more example derived from our anger response:

EI Guide: How can I help you?

Learner: She pissed me off again!

EI Guide: Again? How did she do that this time?

Learner: I was in her room, fixing that broken window we talked about last week, and she looked at me and said, 'You are getting fat.' Can you believe anyone would say that?"

EI Guide: Yes, I can believe it. People are capable of all sorts of behaviors. How was it a problem for you?

Learner: Here we go again. It's a problem for me because I don't like it.

EI Guide: Should people only say things to you that are pleasant and that you like?

Learner: It would be nice.

EI Guide: Sure it would be nice. But is there a law that says they have to?

Learner: Yes, in my head.

EI Guide: What does it mean if someone tells you that you are fat?

Learner: It means I am fat.

EI Guide: How is that a problem for you?

Learner: I don't want to be fat.

EI Guide: What if you are fat?

Learner: Then people will make fun of me.

EI Guide: And . . . ?

Learner: Then I would be a clown?

EI Guide: What would it mean to be a clown?

Learner: It would mean no one would take me seriously.

EI Guide: What if they didn't?

Learner: Then I would be stupid and useless.

EI Guide: All that from someone saying you're fat?

Learner: I guess.

EI Guide: You are pretty hard on yourself.

The Case of Elliot

I chose the following session to illustrate how self-defeating thoughts and behaviors have the potential of interfering with an individual's entire life – unless the issue are addressed early and meaningfully. Please visit http://www.eitheory.com to enhance your reading experience.

****

Background: Elliot is a white, English-speaking, unmarried 17-year-old high school student. Elliot is an only child. He lives with his father, who is an air force chief master sergeant, and his stepmother, who works at the Base Exchange.

Elliot is attending therapy at the request of his stepmother. Elliot recently told his father he is gay, and his father responded by shouting at him, slapping him in the face and telling him he was no longer my son. Elliot's father also told him he was filthy, an abomination, disgusting, a drug addict, a sex fiend and a pedophile. He ordered him out of the house and forbade his wife to ever speak with him again.

Elliot went to his room and his father left the home. His father has been away from home for three days. His stepmother is worried the family is collapsing.

EI Guide: How can I help you?

Elliot: I told my father I was gay and he slapped me and disowned me.

EI Guide: How is that a problem for you?

Elliot: How is a problem? What do you mean, how is it a problem for me? Jesus, how would it be a problem for anyone?

EI Guide: I mean just that. How is your father's rejection of you a problem for you?

Elliot: I wasn't expecting that question.

EI Guide: Then we are off to a good start. How is it a problem for you?

Elliot: I guess it's a problem for me because I want him to accept me.

EI Guide: What does it mean when your father doesn't accept you?

Elliot: This is getting even more confusing.

EI Guide: If your father doesn't care for you, what does it mean?

Elliot: It means he doesn't love me.

EI Guide: Does it mean anything else?

Elliot: It means he doesn't respect me.

EI Guide: Anything else?

Elliot: It means I don't live up to his expectations of me.

EI Guide: Anything else?

Elliot: I think that's about it.

EI Guide: Let's arrange all this information. You told your father you were gay and he rejected you. You took that to mean he doesn't love you; he doesn't respect you and you are not living up to his expectations. Is that correct?

Elliot: Yes. That's about the size of it.

EI Guide: That is what you think.

Elliot: Yes, that is what I think.

EI Guide: What are you feeling?

Elliot: I'm pissed. I'm angry.

EI Guide: Sometimes when we are feeling anger, we are also feeling fear. What are you afraid of?

Elliot: I'm afraid my father thinks I am a piece of shit.

EI Guide: Yes, I can see that. What would it mean if he did?

Elliot: What would it mean? It would mean that I am a piece of shit.

EI Guide: Can it mean anything else?

Elliot: No.

EI Guide: Your father's opinion seems to have the power to turn you into a piece of shit. Yes, I can understand your fear. You don't look like a piece of shit, but I'll take your word for it.

***

Session Two

Elliot: You're making fun of me.

EI Guide: Of course not. But what would it mean if I were?

Elliot: It would mean you don't take me seriously.

EI Guide: Of course I do. But what would it mean it I didn't.

Elliot: This is getting like exercise.

EI Guide: It is like exercise. It's exercising your mind. Play along. What would it mean if I were not taking you seriously, aside from the waste of my time and your money?

Elliot: I guess it would mean that you think I'm a clown.

EI Guide: What if I did think that? What would that mean?

Elliot: I suppose it would mean that I am a joke.

EI Guide: You give me a great deal of power.

Elliot: How so?

EI Guide: If I decide to not take you seriously, that would make you into a clown?

Elliot: I never thought of it that way. I'm not sure I want to agree with you now that you put it that way.

EI Guide: You don't look like a clown, but I can take your word for it.

Elliot: I'm not a clown.

EI Guide: OK, you are not a clown, but you are a piece of shit?

Elliot: I guess.

***

Session Three

EI Guide: So, you are not a clown, but you are a piece of shit?

Elliot: I don't want to be either.

EI Guide: What are we going to do, then?

Elliot: Isn't that your job?

EI Guide: I'm not sure. What do you think my job is?

Elliot: To fix me. To tell me what to think.

EI Guide: You seem to be doing fine telling yourself what to think.

Elliot: I think I'm dizzy.

EI Guide: Let's get back to your father. He doesn't like you to be gay. He has disowned you and shown you disrespect. You believe these events have turned you into a piece of shit. Is that where we are?

Elliot: Yes, I guess.

EI Guide: What does a piece of shit feel like?

Elliot: Oh boy. A piece of shit feels like really depressed and really sad and really scared.

EI Guide: That doesn't sound at all like how I imagined a piece of shit to feel.

Elliot: I'm not really a piece of shit. It is a figure of speech.

EI Guide: Oh, that makes things easier. I was thinking I was going to have to call a plumber.

Elliot: Very funny.

EI Guide: So what we really have with us today is Elliot, a 17-year-old male who is homosexual and who has been rejected by his father and now feels depressed, sad and scared?

Elliot: That about sums it up.

EI Guide: Now we're talking.

***

Session Four

Elliot: I wish I didn't have to be gay. It would make things a lot easier.

EI Guide: What about being gay concerns you?

Elliot: Everything.

EI Guide: Goodness, what motivates you? I mean, if things would have been a lot easier, what compelled you to tell your father you were gay?

Elliot: I wanted to be honest with him and I wanted him to accept me.

EI Guide: What did you imagine being honest and seeking acceptance would bring?

Elliot: Probably exactly what I got.

EI Guide: Then why do it?

Elliot: I think it's best to be honest.

EI Guide: And accepted?

Elliot: Yes, most of all acceptance. People need acceptance.

EI Guide: Do they?

Elliot: Of course they do.

EI Guide: What would it mean if people didn't accept you?

Elliot: It means that I am not acceptable - that there is something wrong with me.

EI Guide: All that from someone not accepting you?

Elliot: Pretty much.

EI Guide: Let me get all this straight. Your father rejects you, and you are a piece of shit? Someone doesn't accept you, and you are unacceptable? That is a lot of power to give to other people. It seems whenever someone thinks something about you, you immediately believe it's true. It's like someone put a spell on you and you become whatever they want you to be. You cannot have happiness in your life unless everyone you meet loves and accepts you?

Elliot: Yes, I suck and you are just telling me how much.

EI Guide: So I have that same kind of control over you?

Elliot: Obviously.

***

Session Five

EI Guide: It must be tough having to go back and forth between being a piece of shit and being unacceptable. What do you suppose we can do about that?

Elliot: You can make me straight.

EI Guide: How do you suppose that would help?

Elliot: People would like me.

EI Guide: Goodness, is that all it takes?

Elliot: Yes. If I were straight, I wouldn't have these particular problems.

EI Guide: Do you think all of your problems would be solved?

Elliot: Not all of them, but most of them.

EI Guide: What about the problems you still have?

Elliot: I could work on those.

EI Guide: You would still have problems?

Elliot: Yes, but not these problems.

EI Guide: Being straight wouldn't solve all your problems?

Elliot: No, I would just have different problems.

EI Guide: How do you suppose we can help you get to the point where you didn't have any problems?

Elliot: I would have to be perfect.

EI Guide: If that's the only way you can be happy with yourself, shall we set that as your goal? To be perfect?

Elliot: Not really. I don't think I will ever be perfect. No one's perfect.

EI Guide: How do you know that?

Elliot: The odds are you will have some problems or that someone won't like you for some reason that isn't under your control. That's just the way things are. No one's perfect. Straight people don't have the same problems as gay people, though.

EI Guide: What kind of problems do straight people have?

Elliot: They don't have to worry about being ridiculed, taunted, rejected and laughed at all the time. People wouldn't be pushing my buttons all the time.

EI Guide: Really? What about a straight person who is obese? How about a straight person who is covered in planters warts? How about a straight person with two heads?

Elliot: That's an extreme example, but I see what you're saying.

EI Guide: I don't think it's a matter of being straight or gay. I think it's what you think about being gay and what you are telling yourself about yourself. When you think about being ridiculed, what are you telling yourself?

Elliot: When my dad ridiculed me, I thought, 'You don't care about me and I can't stand that.'

EI Guide: Anything else?

Elliot: It's funny, but it was like I was looking for him to forgive me for being gay. I said I was looking for acceptance, but I was really looking for forgiveness. I was sort of saying, 'I know this is bad and that I am not perfect, but I want you to forgive me for turning out this way.'

***

Session Six

EI Guide: What do you tell yourself about being gay? I mean, if someone said, 'Elliot, you are a big faggot,' what would you tell yourself?

Elliot: I don't know.

EI Guide: Close your eyes and pay attention to your thoughts. Listen to your self-talk. What are you saying to yourself about that statement?

Elliot: I don't like it. That's for sure.

EI Guide: What about it don't you like?

Elliot: My God, where do I begin?

EI Guide: Listen for words like should, ought, must, have to and need. Look for self-talk that contains those words. Just say whatever comes to your mind.

Elliot: People shouldn't talk to me that way. People should be more courteous. I should be less obvious and not appear to be gay. I should learn to act straight. I should be straight. I thought I was acting straight, but I must not be doing a good job. If I act gay, I am not like everyone else and I a piece of shit. If I act straight I am good. It's my fault that people are making fun of me. Acting gay is bad. If people know I'm gay that means I am not like other people and that is really bad. If someone calls me a faggot, I will have to stand up for myself and fight them. I really don't want to fight people. But if I don't fight them, that makes me a faggot. I don't want to be a faggot, but I don't want to fight. So I am just standing there. I'm not fighting and I am not running. I'm freezing. But I look like a coward and a faggot and there's nothing I can do about it.

EI Guide: That's a lot to think about.

Elliot: You asked for it.

EI Guide: Yes, I did.

Elliot: I never have just listened to my own thoughts, but I am surprised at what I am thinking about. To be honest with you, I think a lot of the fear I have of being viewed as a gay person is that people will confront me and I will have to do something back to them. That really is my big problem. Of course I still think I am a piece of shit anyway. But my biggest problem is that I feel like I have to do something if people make fun of me. I am not really a good fighter. If I say something back, it might cause a fight. It's pretty much a problem with standing up for myself. If I didn't think people would fight me, it would be a different thing altogether.

EI Guide: Is that your only option? Fight or be a coward?

Elliot: I suppose:

EI Guide: Could you do anything else?

Elliot: You can always do something else.

EI Guide: What thoughts would you have to give up, to do something differently – something that you would be happy with doing? If you had one wish that would help handle this situation, what would it be?

Elliot: That they would burst into flames?

EI Guide: That's one option. How about something that is more related to you and your thinking.

Elliot: I'm not sure what to do. That's why I came here. This is sort of the same thing my dad did. He didn't say I was a faggot, but he might as well have.

***

Session Seven

EI Guide: Can you ever be just one thing?

Elliot: I guess not.

EI Guide: You may very well be a combination of a lot of things – both good and not so good.

Elliot: Yes, that's true.

EI Guide: It's one thing to say it's true. It's another thing to believe that it's true.

Elliot: I understand – sort of.

EI Guide: It looks to me like if someone insults you, you make yourself entirely bad. Like when your father rejected you and you became a piece of shit. You all of a sudden became unacceptable. Then our imaginary person called you a faggot, and you became that thing. It's like there is a magic wand that makes you bad. Is there one that makes you good?

Elliot: Yeah, when people praise me. Then I think I'm good.

EI Guide: Until someone tells you you're not?

Elliot: Yes.

EI Guide: You may want to get hold of that. From where I'm sitting, it seems like it would be very exhausting.

Elliot: What do you suggest?

EI Guide: I would suggest that you, first, begin to realize that you are neither good nor bad. You are a number of things, unequal in value and significance. You are too many things to be called by just one name. You can begin to view the things people say to you, both good and not so good, as suggestions. No more than suggestions.

Elliot: So, if someone tells me I am a no good, stinking rotten person - that is a suggestion?

EI Guide: Of course. And it is a suggestion you can either accept or reject. Simply because someone believes this about you is not proof enough that it's true. If someone doesn't like you, is that enough evidence that you are unlikeable? It would be insane for you to believe it anyway. There is overwhelming evidence that it isn't true. It would be insanity to give this statement much more than that - an insane suggestion from a person who appears to have a very little grasp on reality.

Elliot: It's like they're crazy and they are ranting about crazy shit.

EI Guide: That's another way of looking at it. And if you join in with it, you are acting insanely by accepting their insane reality.

***

Session Eight

Elliot: It's sort of like arguing with a crazy person.

EI Guide: Yes, and would you want to fight a crazy person for saying crazy things to you?

Elliot: No. I would probably feel sorry for them.

EI Guide: Let's use that same imagery to understand your father's response to you when you told him you are gay. Is there any connection you can make?

Elliot: My father isn't crazy. He is pretty sane, actually.

EI Guide: Great! But was he saying some crazy stuff to you?

Elliot: Yes. He was saying that gay people are filthy, an abomination, disgusting, drug addicts, sex fiends and pedophiles.

EI Guide: And what is sane about that?

Elliot: Nothing . . . unless I think it's sane to think that.

EI Guide: Is it sane to think you are an abomination filthy, drug addicted, disgusting pedophile?

Elliot: It's pretty insane for someone to think that. I still don't like it.

EI Guide: I'm glad you don't like it. I wouldn't expect you to like it.

Elliot: Well, how do I get rid of my anger?

EI Guide: You can change your thoughts.

Elliot: Like thinking what he's saying is insane?

EI Guide: How would you respond to an insane person who said these things to you?

Elliot: I get it.

EI Guide: Good, but how would you respond? What would you tell yourself?

Elliot: I would tell myself that he doesn't know how to behave. He is hallucinating about something. He is saying things that are crazy and he can't help it.

EI Guide: What emotion would you feel then?

Elliot: I guess I would feel sad. Maybe I would think it was funny.

EI Guide: Shame on you.

Elliot: Is that a suggestion?

EI Guide: Very funny.

***

Session Nine

EI Guide: We're coming to the end of our session. This is where I like to get some feedback, just to make sure we are on the same page, so to speak. Tell me what we talked about today. Or, better yet, tell me what you remember most about our session.

Elliot: Most? I think when you said, 'You cannot have happiness in your life unless you are loved and respected by everyone you meet?'

EI Guide: What about that interests you?

Elliot: Sometimes I think I cannot be as happy as I'd like to be unless people appreciate me and respect me. Like it's the end of the world if someone doesn't like me. I just wish I could do more about that.

EI Guide: It isn't easy, but you can.

Elliot: If you could help me with that, I would really appreciate it.

EI Guide: What do you tell yourself, say, when someone thinks you behaved badly?

Elliot: Tell myself?

EI Guide: Yes, listen to your mind. It will tell you your beliefs. It will tell you what you think of certain things. Let's say someone treated you rudely, say at the convenient store. Say the cashier talked on her cell phone and didn't treat you very well, as a customer. What would you tell yourself about that?

Elliot: I would tell myself she was rude.

EI Guide: And . . . ?

Elliot: She shouldn't be?

EI Guide: And . . . ?

Elliot: She should change.

EI Guide: Why?

Elliot: Because I want her to?

EI Guide: What if she doesn't change?

Elliot: She would be a horrible person and I couldn't stand that.

EI Guide: So you couldn't live happily while she was in the world acting rudely?

Elliot: Now I get it.

EI Guide: If your happiness depends on how well people cooperate with your wishes, you are likely to be unhappy a lot of the time.

Elliot: I get that part, but what can I do instead.

EI Guide: Remember how we talked about viewing the situation differently?

Elliot: About seeing people who act strangely as insane?

EI Guide: Sure. If the cashier were viewed as crazy, emotionally handicapped, what kind of behavior would you expect from her?

Elliot: Crazy?

EI Guide: Should crazy people act any differently?

Elliot: I guess not.

EI Guide: Put that in your own words.

Elliot: I can still be happy in my life, even if people are acting crazy and saying crazy things. I don't have to fight anyone or yell back at them. I can think, 'Boy, this person is really making a lot of poor choices. They are saying all sorts of crazy shit and behaving strangely. I think I should just move away from them.'

EI Guide: What about your thoughts concerning being gay?

Elliot: I guess I still feel like it would be better to be straight. It's easier when you're like other people.

EI Guide: Can you be happy in your life if you're not like other people?

Elliot: Sure I can. I just have to stop thinking that just because someone thinks something bad about me that it's true. I have to give myself my own value, rather than taking everyone's random suggestions of my value. I am in charge of the way I feel because I am in charge of the way I think. If I think differently, I will feel differently. I will never like it that people don't like me because I'm gay, or for any other reason. But I certainly can live my life and be happy. Yes, I think I can do that.

Sandy's Case

EI Guide: How can I help you?

Sandy: I hate being fat.

EI Guide: How is being fat a problem for you?

Sandy: Nobody likes fat people. I am always afraid that someone will make fun of me in public.

EI Guide: Is there anything else about being fat that you don't like?

Sandy: I hate pretending all the time that I am happy being fat.

EI Guide: Anything else?

Sandy: I just hate having to lie all the time and pretend people don't notice how fat I am.

EI Guide: OK . . . anything else?

Sandy: That's about it. I want to be different. I don't want to be this way.

EI Guide: Any of these things more important to you than any other?

Sandy: I guess that everyone hates fat people.

EI Guide: Wow! That's really terrible. How do you know that everyone hates fat people?

Sandy: Because I'm fat and I know. I live through it every day.

EI Guide: Do I hate you?

Dimensions Sandy: I don't know. Do you?

EI Guide: No.

Sandy: How do I know that?

EI Guide: You'll just have to take my word for it.

Sandy: I'm lost.

EI Guide: Yes, let's re-focus. I'm wondering if people generally liked fat people, how you would feel about that.

Sandy: I would be a lot happier.

EI Guide: Would you want to be fat then?

Sandy: Yes. I wouldn't have any problems then.

EI Guide: Would everyone like you then?

Sandy: I guess not. Someone wouldn't like me for some other reason.

EI Guide: I don't think we are talking about you being fat at all.

Sandy: What are we talking about?

EI Guide: Maybe we are talking about how well you accommodate not being liked.

Sandy: Maybe, but I can change myself if people don't like me for other reasons. I mean if people don't like what I'm wearing or what I'm driving, I can change it. I can't change being fat. At least it wouldn't be very easy to do. It would take a lot of something I don't have. I don't want to lose weight. I just want to be liked for who I am.

EI Guide: So if I didn't like your shirt, you would change it?

Sandy: I wouldn't change it, but I wouldn't wear it here again.

EI Guide: What would it mean if I didn't like your shirt?

Sandy: I guess it means you don't like me.

EI Guide: What if I didn't like you?

Sandy: I would feel like I was bad.

EI Guide: Simply because I didn't like your shirt?

Sandy: I guess.

EI Guide: Again, I don't think we're talking about you being fat at all.

Sandy: Goodness. What are we talking about now?

EI Guide: We are talking about you and how much you dislike yourself for any reason anyone can hand to you. We can actually do something about that. Do you want to do something about that?

Sandy: I never really looked at it like that.

EI Guide: What would it mean if someone told you they didn't like you because you were fat?

Sandy: It would mean I couldn't make them like me right away.

EI Guide: And what would it mean to you not to be able to make someone like you right away?

Sandy: I guess I would feel . . . like . . . powerless. Like I would be really off balance until they saw past my fat and liked me.

EI Guide: Is it true that if someone didn't like you because you are fat that you are entirely bad?

Sandy: To them I would be.

EI Guide: That may be. Is it true that you are entirely bad because someone doesn't like your shirt? Your car? Your weight?

Sandy: Not really. I mean it isn't true unless I think it's true.

EI Guide: How do you know it's not true?

Sandy: Because they might not like me, but I have some friends who like me and don't care that I'm fat.

EI Guide: I thought you said EVEYONE hates fat people.

Sandy: I guess I was exaggerating.

EI Guide: It may not be such a good idea to exaggerate when you're in emotional turmoil.

Sandy: True.

EI Guide: So what's so special about the person we are talking about? The one who doesn't like you?

Sandy: I guess I want everyone to like me.

EI Guide: Is it your goal to have everyone like you?

Sandy: I guess.

EI Guide: We may want to work on that goal.

EI Theory Model at a Glance

1. Recognize that your emotional response is ***unmanageable***.
2. ***Commit*** to emotional evolution.
3. ***Articulate*** the problem.
4. ***Articulate*** the question, "How is this issue a problem for me?"
5. ***Identify*** words that dictate your ***absolute terms of engagement***, i.e., ***should, ought, must, have to and need***.
6. ***Articulate***, "What does it mean to me to be treated contrary to how I demand?"
   a. If I am treated disrespectfully, carelessly, irresponsibly, etc., and I think I ***should not be***, it means that I am not worthy of respect, love, care, affection, etc.
   b. Articulate, "Where is the proof that my demands are facts. Where is the proof that my demands are anything but products of my imagination?"
   c. There is no proof that my happiness, self-image, self-acceptance, vision on my future depends on how this person is treating me?
   d. There is proof that I am not getting what I want. I don't have to think of it in terms of demands, only wants. I don't always get what I want. I can forgive, feel sad for or just be less angry about how this person is behaving. I can make that choice by telling myself something more reasonable than what I am telling myself now. I will not be happy that people behave this way, but I can be more forgiving and less critical of people who choose to behave poorly. Their behavior

has little to nothing to do with how I will feel about it. I make that choice.

Bibliography

Abrams, M & Abrams, L.: A Brief Biography of Dr. Albert Ellis 1913–2007

Antonakis, J. (2009). "Emotional intelligence": What does it measure and does it matter for leadership?. In G. B. Graen (Ed). LMX leadership--Game-Changing Designs: Research-Based Tools (Vol. VII) (pp. 163-192). Greenwich, CT: Information Age Publishing. Download article: [1], link to book: http://www.infoagepub.com/products/Predators-Game-Changing-Designs

Antonakis, J., & Dietz, J. (2011a). Looking for Validity or Testing It? The Perils of Stepwise Regression, Extreme-Scores Analysis, Heteroscedasticity, and Measurement Error. Personality and Individual Differences, 50(3), 409-415, http://dx.doi.org/10.1016/j.paid.2010.09.014

Antonakis, J., & Dietz, J. (2011b). More on Testing for Validity Instead of Looking for It. Personality and Individual Differences, 50(3), 418-421, http://dx.doi.org/10.1016/j.paid.2010.10.008

Antonakis, J.; Ashkanasy, N. M.; Dasborough, M. (2009). "Does leadership need emotional intelligence?". The Leadership Quarterly 20 (2): 247–261. doi:10.1016/j.leaqua.2009.01.006.

Austin, E.J. (2008). A reaction time study of responses to trait and ability emotional intelligence test items. Personality and Individual Differences, 36, 1855-1864.

Bar-On, Reuven; Parker, James DA (2000). The Handbook of Emotional Intelligence: Theory, Development, Assessment, and Application at Home, School, and in the Workplace. San

Francisco, California: Jossey-Bass. ISBN 0787949841. pp. 40-59

Bar-On, R. (1997). The Emotional Quotient Inventory (EQ-i): a test of emotional intelligence. Toronto: Multi-Health Systems.

Bar-On, R. (2006). The Bar-On model of emotional-social intelligence (ESI). Psicothema, 18 , supl., 13-25.

Boyatzis, R., Goleman, D., & Rhee, K. (2000). Clustering competence in emotional intelligence: insights from the emotional competence inventory (ECI). In R. Bar-On & J.D.A.

Bradberry, Travis and Greaves, Jean. (2009). Emotional Intelligence 2.0. San Francisco: Publishers Group West. ISBN 9780974320625

Brody, N. (2004). What cognitive intelligence is and what emotional intelligence is not. Psychological Inquiry, 15, 234-238. Schulte, M. J., Ree, M. J., & Carretta, T. R. (2004). Emotional intelligence: Not much more than g and personality. Personality and Individual Differences, 37, 1059–1068, http://dx.doi.org/10.1016/j.paid.2003.11.014

Cornwall, M. (2008). Using articulated thought disputation (ATD) to strengthen rational emotive behavior theory (REBT). Northcentral University, 2008 ISBN 0549611142, 9780549611141.

Cornwall, M. (2010). *Go suck a lemon.*

Cote, S. and Miners, C.T.H. (2006). "Emotional intelligence, cognitive intelligence and job performance", Administrative Science Quarterly, 51(1), pp1-28. Retrieved from http://en.wikipedia.org/w/index.php?title=Emotional_intelligence&oldid=455756959

Ellis, A. & Abrams, M. (2008). Personality Theories: Critical Perspectives.
    Thousand Oaks, Ca.:Sage Publications.

Ellis, A. (1964) if this be heresy... Is pornography harmful to children? In
    The Realist No.47 pp.17-8, 23

Ellis A. (2000). Can rational emotive behavior therapy (REBT) be effectively used with people who have devout beliefs in God and religion?. Professional Psychology: Research and Practice, 31(1), Feb 2000. pp. 29–33

Eysenck, H.J. (2000). Intelligence: A New Look. ISBN 0765807076 Locke, E.A. (2005). "Why emotional intelligence is an invalid concept". Journal of Organizational Behavior 26 (4): 425–431. doi:10.1002/job.318.

Farley, F. (2009). Albert Ellis (1913–2007). American Psychologist, Vol
    64(3), pp. 215–216

Fiori, M., & Antonakis, J. (2011). The ability model of emotional intelligence: Searching for valid measures. Personality and Individual Differences, 50(3), 329-334, http://dx.doi.org/10.1016/j.paid.2010.10.010

Gardner, H. (1983). Frames of mind. New York: Basic Books.

Gardner, J. K.; Qualter, P. (2010). "Concurrent and incremental validity of three trait emotional intelligence measures". Australian Journal of Psychology 62: 5–12. doi:10.1080/00049530903312857.

Goleman, D. (1998). Working with emotional intelligence. New York: Bantam Books

Hans, T. (2000). A meta-analysis of the effects of adventure programming on locus of control. Journal of Contemporary Psychotherapy, 30(1),33-60.

Harms, P. D.; Credé, M. (2010). "Remaining Issues in Emotional Intelligence Research: Construct Overlap, Method Artifacts, and Lack of Incremental Validity". Industrial and Organizational Psychology: Perspectives on Science and Practice 3 (2): 154–158. doi:10.1111/j.1754-9434.2010.01217.x.

Harms, P. D.; Credé, M. (2010). "Emotional Intelligence and Transformational and Transactional Leadership: A Meta-Analysis". Journal of Leadership & Organizational Studies 17 (1): 5–17. doi:10.1177/1548051809350894. http://digitalcommons.unl.edu/cgi/viewcontent.cgi?article=1013&context=leadershipfacpub.

Hattie, J. A., Marsh, H. W., Neill, J. T. & Richards, G. E. (1997). Adventure Education and Outward Bound: Out-of-class experiences that have a lasting effect. Review of Educational Research, 67, 43-87.

Kluemper, D.H. (2008) Trait emotional intelligence: The impact of core-self evaluations and social desirability. Personality and Individual Differences, 44(6), 1402-1412.

Korzybski A. (1933). Science and Sanity. Institute of General Semantics,

1994, ISBN 0-937298-01-8

Landy, F.J. (2005). Some historical and scientific issues related to research

on emotional intelligence. Journal of Organizational Behavior,

26, 411-424.

Leuner, B. (1966). Emotional intelligence and emancipation. Praxis der Kinderpsychologie und Kinderpsychiatrie, 15, 193-203.

Mamlin, N., Harris, K. R., Case, L. P. (2001). A Methodological Analysis
of Research on Locus of Control and Learning Disabilities: Rethinking a Common Assumption. Journal of Special Education, Winter.

Marsh, H. W. & Richards, G. E. (1986). The Rotter Locus of Control Scale: The comparison of alternative response formats and implications for reliability, validity and dimensionality. Journal of Research in Personality, 20, 509-558.

Marsh, H. W. & Richards, G. E. (1987). The multidimensionality of the Rotter I-E Scale and its higher order structure: An application of confirmatory factor analysis. Multivariate Behavioral Research, 22, 39-69.

Martins, A.; Ramalho, N.; Morin, E. (2010). "A comprehensive meta-analysis of the relationship between emotional intelligence and health". Journal of Personality and Individual Differences 49 (6): 554–564. doi:10.1016/j.paid.2010.05.029.

Mattiuzzi, P.G. Emotional Intelligence? I'm not feeling it. everydaypsychology.com

Mayer, J.D., Salovey, P., Caruso, D.R., & Sitarenios, G. (2003). Measuring emotional intelligence with the MSCEIT V2.0. Emotion, 97-105.

http://www.psykologi.uio.no/studier/drpsych/disputaser/follesdal_summary.html Hallvard Føllesdal - 'Emotional Intelligence as Ability: Assessing the Construct Validity of Scores from the

Mayer-Salovey-Caruso Emotional Intelligence Test (MSCEIT)' PhD Thesis and accompanying papers, University of Oslo 2008

Mayer, J.D., Salovey, P., Caruso, D.L., & Sitarenios, G. (2001). Emotional intelligence as a standard intelligence. Emotion, 1, 232-242.

Mayer, J.D., & Salovey, P. (1997). What is emotional intelligence? In P. Salovey & D. Sluyter (Eds.), Emotional development and emotional intelligence: Implications for educators (pp. 3-31). New York: Basic Books.

Mikolajczak, M., Luminet, O., Leroy, C., & Roy, E. (2007). Psychometric properties of the Trait Emotional Intelligence Questionnaire. Journal of Personality Assessment, 88, 338-353.

Mikolajczak, Luminet, Leroy, and Roy (2007). Psychometric Properties of the Trait Emotional Intelligence Questionnaire: Factor Structure, Reliability, Construct, and Incremental Validity in a French-Speaking Population. Journal of Personality Assessment, 88(3), 338–353

Nielsen, Stevan Lars & Ellis, Albert. (1994). A discussion with Albert Ellis: Reason, emotion and religion, Journal of Psychology and Christianity, 13(4), Win 1994. pp. 327–341

Palovey, P., & Mayer, J.D. (1990). Emotional intelligence. Imagination, Cognition, and Personality, 9, 185-211.

Parker, JDA; Taylor, GJ; Bagby, RM (2001). "The Relationship Between Emotional Intelligence and Alexithymia". Personality and Individual Differences 30: 107–115. doi:10.1016/S0191-8869(00)00014-3.

Payne, W.L. (1983/1986). A study of emotion: developing emotional intelligence; self integration; relating to fear, pain and desire.

Dissertation Abstracts International, 47, p. 203A (University microfilms No. AAC 8605928)

Petrides, K.V. & Furnham, A. (2000a). On the dimensional structure of emotional intelligence. Personality and Individual Differences, 29, 313-320

Petrides, K.V., Pita, R., Kokkinaki, F. (2007). The location of trait emotional intelligence in personality factor space. British Journal of Psychology, 98, 273-289.

Petrides, K.V. & Furnham, A. (2001). Trait emotional intelligence: Psychometric investigation with reference to established trait taxonomies. European Journal of Personality, 15, 425-448

Pérez, J.C., Petrides, K.V., & Furnham, A. (2005). Measuring trait emotional intelligence. In R. Schulze and R.D. Roberts (Eds.), International Handbook of Emotional Intelligence (pp.181-201). Cambridge, MA: Hogrefe & Huber.

Petrides, K.V., & Furnham, A. (2003). Trait emotional intelligence: behavioral validation in two studies of emotion recognition and reactivity to mood induction. European Journal of Personality, 17, 39–75

Prospect Magazine: Albert Ellis. August 1, 2007 Issue 137 Jules Evans New York Times: Albert Ellis, Influential Psychotherapist, Dies at 93 psychotherapy.net: An Interview with Albert Ellis, PhD Rational Emotive Behavioral Therapy

Roberts, R.D., Zeidner, M., & Matthews, G. (2001). Does emotional intelligence meet traditional standards for an intelligence? Some new data and conclusions. Emotion, 1, 196–231

Rotter, J. (1966). Generalized expectancies for internal versus external control of reinforcements. Psychological Monographs, 80, Whole No. 609.

Salovey P and Grewal D (2005) The Science of Emotional Intelligence. Current directions in psychological science, Volume 14 -6 Bradberry, T. and Su, L. (2003). Ability-versus skill-based assessment of emotional intelligence, Psicothema, Vol. 18, supl., pp. 59-66.

Smith, M.K. (2002) "Howard Gardner and multiple intelligences", The Encyclopedia of Informal Education, downloaded from http://www.infed.org/thinkers/gardner.htm on October 31, 2005.

Smith, L., Ciarrochi, J., & Heaven, P. C. L., (2008). The stability and change of trait emotional intelligence, conflict communication patterns, and relationship satisfaction: A one-year longitudinal study. Personality and Individual Differences, 45, 738-743.

Thorndike, R.K. (1920). "Intelligence and Its Uses", Harper's Magazine 140, 227-335.

Taylor, Graeme J; Bagby, R. Michael and Parker, James DA (1997). Disorders of Affect Regulation: Alexithymia in Medical and Psychiatric Illness. Cambridge: Cambridge University Press. ISBN 052145610X. pp. 28-31

William Knaus, Jon Geis, Ed Garcia. A Message in Support of Dr. Albert
    Ellis from Three Former Directors of Training of the Albert Ellis
    Institute

Vernon, P.A.; Petrides, K.V.; Bratko, D.; Schermer, J.A. (2008). "A behavioral genetic study of trait emotional intelligence". Emotion 8 (5): 635–642. doi:10.1037/a0013439. PMID 18837613.

Vorst, HCM; Bermond, B (2001). "Validity and reliability of the Bermond-Vorst Alexithymia Questionnaire". Personality and Individual Differences 30 (3): 413–434. doi:10.1016/S0191-8869(00)00033-7.

Yankura J. & Dryden W. (1994). Albert Ellis. SAGE. Recollection of Stevan Lars Nielsen, Ph.D. who was present at the 90th birthday party The New Yorker: The Human Condition – Ageless, Guiltless NY Courts: Ellis v Broder (2006 NY Slip Op 26023)

References particular to Articulated Thought and Rational Social Problem Solving

Aguilar, N. (1997). Counseling the learner with chronic illness: Strategies for thehealthcare provider. *Journal of American Academy of Nurse Practitioners. 9*(4), 171-5.

Anderson, J. (2002). Executive coaching and REBT: Some comments from the field. *Journal of Rational - Emotive & Cognitive - Behavior Therapy, 20*(3-4), 223. Retrieved July 30, 2007, from ProQuest Psychology Journals database. (Document ID: 386245661).

Aristotle (350 BC). The nicomachean ethics. Retrieved May, 12, 2006, from http://www.ilt.columbia.edu/publicATIONS/artistotle.html

Aviv, R. (2005). The interpretation of reams. Retrieved September 12, 2006 from http://www.villagevoice.com/people/0534,interview,67068,24.html

Beck, A. (1994). Foreword. In Kingdon & Turkington (Eds.), Cognitive-behavioral therapy of schizophrenia (pp. v-vii). New York: Guilford Press.

Berger, V. (2005). Rational emotive behavior therapy. Retrieved August 10, 2007, from http://www.psychologistanywhereanytime.com/treatment_and_therapy_psychologist/psychologist_rational_emotive_behavioral_therapy.htm

Bernard, M., & Wolfe, J. (2000). The RET resource book for practitioners. New York: Institute for Rational-Emotive Therapy.

Berne, J. (2004). Think-aloud protocol and adult learners. *Adult Basic Education, 14*(3), 153-173.

Besser, A., Flett, G., & Hewitt, P. (2004). Perfectionism, cognition, and affect in response to performance failure to success. *Journal of Rational-Emotive & Cognitive Behavior Therapy, 22*(4).

Biggam F., & Power K. (1999). Social Problem Solving skills and psychological distress among incarcerated young offenders: The issue of bullying and victimisation. *Cognitive Therapy and Research, 23*, 307-326.

Bishop, W., & Fish J. (1999). Questions as interventions: Perceptions of Socratic, solution focused, and diagnostic questioning styles. *Journal of Rational-Emotive and Cognitive-Behavior Therapy, 17*(2), 115-140.

Blankstein, K., & Winkworth, G. (2004). Dimensions of perfectionism and levels of attributions for grades:

Relations with dysphoria and academic performance. *Journal of Rational-Emotive & Cognitive Behavior Therapy, 22*(4).

Boelen, P., & Baars, L. (2004). Two studies on the psychometric properties of the belief scale. *Gedragstherapie, 37*(4).

Boelen, P., Kip, H., & Voorsluijs, J. (2004). Irrational beliefs and basic assumptions in bereaved university students: A comparison study. *Journal of Rational-Emotive & Cognitive Behavior Therapy, 22*(2).

Bransford, J., & Stein, B. (1984). The IDEAL problem solver. New York: W. H. Freeman.

Broder, M. (2001). Dr. Albert Ellis – Ellis in his own words – On success. *Journal of Rational – Emotive & Cognitive - Behavior Therapy, 19*(2), 77. Retrieved September 6, 2006, from ProQuest Psychology Journals database. (Document ID: 386235861).

Broder, M. (2000). Making optimal use of homework to enhance your therapeutic effectiveness. *Journal of Rational Emotive and Cognitive Behavior Therapy, 8*(1), 3-18.

Byrne, J. (2006). Research issues in coaching, counseling, and psychotherapy. Some ideas and developments. Retrieved February 12, 2006, from http://rebt.cc/_wsn/page12.html

Chang, E., D'Zurilla, T., & Sanna, L. (2004). Social Problem Solving: theory, research, and training. APA: Washington, D.C.

Chang, E., D'Zurilla, T., & Maydeu-Olivares, A. (1994). Assessing the dimensionality of optimism and pessimism using a multimeasure approach. *Cognitive Therapy and*

Research, 18, 143-160.

Clark, D. (1999). Constructivism. Retrieved September 15, 2007, from http://www.nwlink.com/~donclark/hrd/history/history.html

Collins, A., Brown, J., & Newman, S. (1989). Cognitive apprenticeship: Teaching the crafts of reading, writing, and mathematics. In L. B. Resnick (Ed.). Knowing, learning and instruction: Essays in honor of Robert Glaser (pp. 453-494). Hillsdale, NJ: Lawrence Erlbaum Associates.

Corsini, R., & Wedding, D. (1995). Current Psychotherapies. Itasca, Illinois: F.E. Peacock Publishers.

Criddle, W. (2007). The transition from therapist to executive coach. *Journal of Rational-Emotive & Cognitive-Behavior Therapy (25)*2, 121-141.

D'Zurilla, T., Nezu, A., & Maydeu-Olivares, A. (2002). Social Problem Solving Inventory-Revised (Social Problem Solving – R). North Tonawanda, NY: Multi-Health Systems, Inc.

D'Zurilla, T., & Nezu, A. (1999). Problem Solving therapy: A social competence approach to clinical intervention (2nd ed.). New York: Springer.

D'Zurilla, T., & Maydeu-Olivares, A. (1995). Conceptual and methodological issues in Social Problem Solving assessment. *Behavior Therapy, 26*, 409-432.

D'Zurilla, T. J. (1986). Problem Solving therapy: A social competence approach to clinical intervention. New York: Springer Publishing Co.

D'Zurilla, T. J., & Nezu, A. (1982). Social Problem Solving in adults. In P. C. Kendall (Ed.), Advances in cognitive-behavioral research and therapy. New York: Academic Press.

D'Zurilla, T., & Godfried, M. (1971). Problem Solving and behavior modification. *Journal of Abnormal Psychology, 78*, 107-26.

David, D. and Avellino, M. (2002) A Synopsis of REBT Research: Basic/Fundemental and Applied Research. Retrieved February 11, 2006, from http://rebt.cc/db5/00479/rebt.cc/_download/ASYNOPSISOFRebtRESEARCH.doc

David, D., Macavei, B., & Szentagotai, A. (2005). Cognitive restructuring and mental contamination: An empirical re-conceptualization. *Journal of Rational-Emotive & Cognitive-Behavior Therapy, 23*, 1, 21-55.

David, D., Szentagotai, A., Eva, K., & Macavei, B. (2005). A synopsis of rational-emotive behavior therapy (REBT): Fundamental and applied research. *Journal of Rational – Emotive & Cognitive - Behavior Therapy, 23*(3), 175-221. Retrieved September 4, 2006, from ProQuest Psychology Journals database. (Document ID: 997217251).

Davidson, G., Vogel, R., & Coffman, S. (1997). Think-aloud approaches to cognitive assessment and articulated thoughts in simulated situations paradigm. *Journal of Consulting and Clinical Psychology, 65*(6), 950-958.

Davison, G., Robins, C., & Johnson, M. (1983). Articulated thoughts during simulated situations: A paradigm for studying cognition in emotion and behavior. *Cognitive Therapy and Research, 7*, 17-40.

DiLiberto, L., Katz, R., Beauchamp, K., & Howells, G. (2002).

Using articulated thoughts in simulated situations to assess cognitive activity in aggressive and nonaggressive adolescents. *Journal of Child and Family Studies, 11,*(2), 179-189.

Dryden, W. (2007). My idiosyncratic practice of REBT. Retrieved May, 4, 2007 from, http://www.psychotherapy.ro/index2.php?option=com_content&do_pdf=1&id=30

Dryden, W. (2005). Rational emotive behavior therapy. In: Comparative treatments for borderline personality disorder. Freeman, A., Stone, M. & Martin, D. (2005) New York: Springer Publishing Co.

Dryden, W., & Neenan, M. (2003). The REBT therapist's pocket companion. Retrieved January 4, 2007, from http://www.walden3.org/Pocket%20REBT%204%20Therapists.pdf

Dryden, W., Ferguson, J., & Clark, T. (1989). Beliefs and inferences: A test of rational-emotive hypothesis 1. Performing in an academic seminar. Journal of Rational-Emotive and Cognitive-Behavior Therapy, 7, 119–129.

Du Plessis, M., Möller, A., & Steel, H. (2004). The Irrational Beliefs Inventory: Cross-cultural comparisons between South African and previously published Dutch and American samples. *Psychological Reports, 95*(3, Part1). (Document ID: 386245621).

Dyer, W. (1977). Erroneous Zones. New York: Avon.

Eckhardt, C., & Jamison, T. (2002). Articulated thoughts of male perpetrators of dating violence during anger arousal.

Cognitive Therapy and Research, 26, 289-308.

Eckhardt, C., Barbour, K., & Davison, G. (1998). Articulated irrational thoughts in maritally violent and nonviolent men during anger arousal. *Journal of Consulting and Clinical Psychology, 66*, 259-269.

Ellis, A. (2003a). Early theories and practices of rational emotive behavior therapy and how they have been augmented and revised during the last three decades. *Journal of Rational - Emotive & Cognitive - Behavior Therapy: Albert Ellis' 90th Birthday Celebration: His Contribution, 21*. Retrieved September 9, 2006, from, ProQuest Psychology Journals database. (Document ID: 424411351).

Ellis, A. (2003b). The relationship of rational emotive behavior therapy (REBT) to Social Psychology. *Journal of Rational - Emotive & Cognitive - Behavior Therapy, 21*(1), 5. Retrieved September 2, 2006, from ProQuest Psychology Journals database. (Document ID: 440142431).

Ellis, A. (2003c). Early theories and practices of rational emotive behavior theory and how they have been augmented and revised during the last three decades. *Journal of Rational-Emotive & Cognitive-Behavior Therapy, 21*(3/4).

Ellis, A., & Joffe, D. (2002). A study of volunteer learners who experienced live sessions of rational emotive behavior therapy in front of a public audience. *Journal of Rational - Emotive & Cognitive - Behavior Therapy, 20*(2), 151.

Retrieved September 2, 2006, from ProQuest database. (Document ID: 386235871).

Ellis, A. (2001). Feeling better, getting better, staying better. New York: Impact Publishers, 2001. ISBN 1-886230-35-8.

Ellis, A. (2001). Reasons why rational emotive behavior therapy is relatively neglected in the professional and scientific literature: *Journal of Rational-Emotive and Cognitive-Behavior Therapy, 19*(1), 67-74.

Ellis, A., & Grieger, R. (1997). Handbook of Rational-Emotive Therapy. New York: Springer Publishing Co.

Ellis, A., & Harper, R. (1997). A guide to rational living (3rd ed.). Hollywood, CA: Wilshire.

Ellis, A. (1995). Changing rational-emotive therapy (RET) to rational emotive behavior therapy (REBT). *Journal of Rational-Emotive & Cognitive-Behavior Therapy, 3*(2).

Ellis, A., & Dryden, W. (1987). The practice of rational-emotive therapy. New York: Springer.

Ellis, A. (1950). An introduction to the principles of scientific psychoanalysis. *Genetic Psychology Monographs, 41*.

Ellis, A., Eisenbud, J. Pederson-Krag, G. & Fodor, N. (1947). Telepathy and psychoanalysis: A critique of recent "findings". *Journal Psychiatric Quarterly, 21*(4), 607-631.

Ellis, A., & Conrad, H. (1946). The validity of personality questionnaires. *Psychological Bulletin, 43*.

Emerson, R. (1841). Self reliance. Retrieved September 5, 2007, from http://www.smartwomeninvest.com/emerson.pdf

Engels, G., Garnefski, N., & Diekstra, R. (1993). Efficacy of rational-emotive therapy: A quantitative analysis. *Journal of Consulting and Clinical Psychology, 61*(6), 1083. Retrieved September 4, 2006, from PsycARTICLES database. (Document ID: 293526571).

Fenichel, M. (2000). Asynchronously live from APA 2000. Retrieved September 2, 2006 from http://www.fenichel.com/Beck-Ellis.shtml

Flanagan, R., Povall, L., Dellino, M., & Byrne, L. (1998). A comparison of problem solving with and without rational emotive behavior therapy to improve children's social skills. *Journal of Rational-Emotive & Cognitive-Behavior Therapy, 16*(2), 125-134.

Friedberg, R., Miller, R., Perymon, A., Bottoms, J., & Aatre, G. (2004). Using a session feedback form in cognitive therapy with children. *Journal of Rational - Emotive & Cognitive - Behavior Therapy, 22*(3), 219-230. Retrieved August 27, 2007, from ProQuest Psychology Journals database. (Document ID: 817362381).

Froggart, W. (2005). Rational emotive behaviour therapy. Retrieved September 3, 2006, from http://www.rational.org.nz/prof/docs/Intro-REBT.pdf#search=%22rebt%20biopsychosocial%22

Froggatt, Wayne (2005). A brief introduction to rational emotive behaviour therapy. 3rd Edition, New Zealand: Centre for Cognitive Behaviour Therapy.

Gateley, G. (1999). Rational-behavior therapy as correcting demamaps. *et Cetera, 56*(3), 274-279. Retrieved January 24, 2007, from Research Library database. (Document ID: 46562130).

Glaser, N., Kazantzis, N., Deane, F., & Oades, L. (2000). Critical issues in using homework assignments within cognitive behavioural therapy for schizophrenia. *Journal of National-Emotive and Cognitive-Behavior Therapy. 18*(4), 247-261.

Gonzalez, J., Nelson, J., & Gutkin, T. (2005). Rational emotive therapy with children and adolescents: A meta-analysis. *Journal of Emotional & Behavioral Disorders, 12*(4).

Gazzaniga, M. (2006) Leon Festinger. Lunch with Leon. *Perspectives on Psychological Science 1* (1), 88–94.

Gossette, R., & O'Brien, R. (1993). Efficacy of rational emotive therapy (RET) with children: A critical reappraisal. *Journal of Behavior Therapy and Experimental Psychology, 24*, 15-25.

Greeno, J. (1997). On claims that answer the wrong questions. *Educational Researcher, 26*(1), 5-17.

Guterman, J., & Rudes, J. (2005). A solution-focused approach to rational-emotive behavior therapy: toward a theoretical integration. *Journal of Rational – Emotive & Cognitive - Behavior Therapy, 23*(3), 223-244. Retrieved August 27, 2007, from ProQuest Psychology Journals database. (Document ID: 997217241).

Haaga, D., & Davison, G. (1993). An appraisal of rational-emotive therapy. *Journal of Consulting and Clinical Psychology, 61*, 215-220.

Haaga, D., & Davison, G. (1989). Slow progress in rational-emotive therapy outcome research: Etiology and treatment. *Cognitive Therapy and Research, 13*, 493-508.

Haaga, D., & Stewart, B. (1992). Self-efficacy for recovery from a lapse after smoking cessation. *Journal of Consulting and Clinical Psychology, 60*, 24-28.

Halasz, G. (2004) In conversation with Dr Albert Ellis. *Australasian Psychiatry, 12*(4).

Hauck, P. (2001). When Reason Is Not Enough. *Journal of Rational-Emotive and Cognitive-Behavior Therapy, 19*(4), 245-257.

Heery, M. (2000). An interview with Albert Ellis, PhD. Retrieved August 5, 2006 from http://www.psychotherapy.net/interview/Albert_Ellis

Huitt, W. (1992). Problem Solving and decision making: Consideration of individual differences using the Myers-Briggs Type Indicator. *Journal of Psychological Type*, 24, 33-44.

Hurley, D. (2004). From therapy's Lenny Bruce: Get over it! Stop whining! Retrieved October 1, 2006 from, http://www.rebt.ws/recentarticles.html

Johnson, M., & Kazantzis, N. (2004). Cognitive behavioral therapy for chronic pain: Strategies for the successful use of homework assignments. *Journal of Rational-Emotive & Cognitive-Behaviour Therapy. 22*(3), 189-218.

Johnson, W. (2005). Rational emotive behavior therapy for disturbance about sexual orientation. In: Casebook for a spiritual strategy in counseling and psychotherapy.

Jones, R. (1968). A factorial measure of Ellis's irrational belief system. Unpublished doctoral dissertation.Texas Technological College .

Kahn, B., & Kahn, W. (2001). Is REBT marginalized? A survey

of counselor educators. *Journal of Rational - Emotive & Cognitive - Behavior Therapy, 19*(1), 5. Retrieved September 18, 2006, from ProQuest Psychology Journals database. (Document ID: 386235771).

Kanter, J. (1988). Clinical issues in the case management relationship. *New Directions for Mental Health Services,* 40, 15-27.

Kendall, P. (1984). Cognitive processes and procedures in behavior therapy. In T.G. Wilson, C.M. Franks, K.P. Brownell, & P.C. Kendall (eds.), Annual review of behavior therapy (pp. 123-164). New York: Guilford Press.

Keyes, K. (1997). Handbook to Higher Consciousness. Arrojo Rande: Love Line Books.

Kinney, A. (2000). The intellectual-insight problem: Implications for assessment and rational-emotive behavior therapy. *Journal of Contemporary Psychotherapy, 30*(3), 261. Retrieved January 11, 2007, from ProQuest Psychology Journals database. (Document ID: 386244251).

Kucan, L., & Beck, I. (1997). Thinking aloud and reading comprehension research:Inquiry, instruction, and social interaction. Review of Educational Research, 67,271–299.

Lodge, J., Tripp, G., & Harte, D. (2000). Think-aloud, thought-listing, and video-mediated recall procedures in assessment of children's self-talk. *Cognitive Therapy and Research, 24*(4), 399-418.

McCown, W., & Carlson, G. (2004). Narcissism, perfectionism

and self-termination from treatment in outlearner cocaine users. *Journal of Rational-Emotive & Cognitive Behavior Therapy, 22*(4).

McDermut, J. F., Haaga, A. A. F., & Bilek, L. A. (1997). Cognitive bias and irrational beliefs in major depression and dysphoria. Cognitive Therapy and Research, 21, 459–476.

Macavei, B. (2005). The role of irrational beliefs in the rational emotive behavior theory of depression. *Journal of Cognitive & Behavioral Psychotherapies, 5*(1).

Mahoney, M. (2004). What is constructivism and why is it growing? *Contemporary Psychology*, 49, 360-363.

Marini, A., & Genereux, R. (1995). The challenge of teaching for transfer. In A. McKeough, J. Lupart, & A. Marini (Eds.), Teaching for transfer: Fostering generalization in learning (pp. 1-19). Mahwah, NJ: Lawrence Erlbaum Associates.

Martin-Hanson, L. & Johnson, J. (2006). Think-aloud in inquiry science. *Scienceand Children, 44*(1), 56-59.

Mulhauser, G. (2007). An introduction to rational emotive behavior therapy. Retrieved January 3, 2007, from http://counsellingresource.com/types/rational-emotive/index.html

Neenan, M. (2001). REBT 45 Years on: Still on the sidelines. *Journal of Rational – Emotive & Cognitive - Behavior Therapy, 19*(1), 31. Retrieved September 18, 2006, from ProQuest Psychology Journals database. (Document ID: 386235751).

Neenan, M. (1999). Problem-creating to Problem Solving.

Retrieved March 3, 2006, from http://www.isma.org.uk/stressnw/problems.htm

Nielsen, S. (2004). A Mormon rational emotive behavior therapist attempts qur'anic rational emotive behavior therapy. In: Casebook for a spiritual strategy in counseling and psychotherapy. Richards, P. (2004). Dept of Counseling Psychology & Special Education, Brigham Young University. Washington, DC: American Psychological Association.

Overholser, J. (2003). Rational-emotive behavior therapy: An interview withAlbert Ellis. *Journal of Contemporary Psychotherapy, 33*(3), 187.Retrieved September 2, 2006, from ProQuest Psychology Journals database. (Document ID: 348759781).

Palmer, S. (1997). A rational emotive behavior approach to hypnosis. The Rational Emotive Behavior Therapist, 5, 1, 34-54.

Pedersen, S., & Liu, M. (2003). The transfer of Problem Solving skills from a problem-based learning environment: The effect of modeling an expert's cognitive processes. *Journal on Technology in Education, 35*(2), 303-320.

Pedersen, S., & Liu, M. (2002). The transfer of Problem Solving skills from a problem-based learning environment: The effect of modeling an expert's cognitive processes. *Journal of Research on Technology in Education. 35*(2), 303-320.

Polya, G. (1971). How to solve it. Princeton, NJ: Princeton University Press.Popa, S. (2001). Interview with Albert Ellis: The "cognitive revolution" inpsychotherapy.

Romanian Journal of Cognitive and Behavioural Psycho therapies, 1, 7-17.

Rayburn, N., & Davison, G. (2002). Articulated thoughts about antigay hate crimes. *Journal Cognitive Therapy and Research, 26*(4), 431-447. Reinhard, J. (2000). Limitations of mental health case management: A rational emotive and cognitive therapy perspective. *Journal of Rational - Emotive & Cognitive – Behavior Therapy, 18*(2), 103. Retrieved August 27, 2007, from ProQuest Psychology Journals database. (Document ID: 386235821).

Robb, H., Backx, W., & Thomas, J. (1999). The use of cognitive, emotive and behavioral interventions in rational emotive behavior therapy when learners lack emotional insight. *Journal of Rational-Emotive & Cognitive-behaviorTherapy, 17*, 201-209.

Robertson, D. (2001). REBT, philosophy and philosophical counseling. Retrieved June 22, 2006, from http://www.practical-philosophy.org.uk/Volume3Articles/REBT.htm

Rorer, L. (1999). Dealing with the intellectual-insight problem in cognitive and rational emotive behavior therapy. *Journal of Rational - Emotive & Cognitive - Behavior Therapy, 17*(4), 217. Retrieved January 5, 2007, from ProQuest Psychology Journals database. (Document ID: 337476351).

Salsbery, K. (2005). [Review of the book Rational Emotive Behavior Therapy: It Works for Me -- It Can Work for You]. Retrieved November 7, 2006, from http://mentalhelp.net/poc/view_doc.php?id=2711&type=book&cn=91

Savron, G., Bartolucci, G. & Pitti, A. (2004). Psychopathological modification after cognitive behaviour treatment of obsessive-compulsive learners. *Rivista di Psichiatria, 39*(3).

Schuster, S. (1999). Philosophical counseling and rationality. Retrieved June 2, 2007, from http://www.geocities.com/centersophon/press/ox99.html

Smith, M., Glass, G., & Miller, T. (1980). The benefits of psychotherapy. Baltimore: Johns Hopkins University Press.

Smith, M., & Glass, G. (1977). Meta-analysis of psychotherapy outcome studies. American Psychologist, 32, 752-760.

Solomon, A., Bruce, A., Gotlib, I. H., & Wind, B. (2003). Individualized measurement of irrational beliefs in remitted depressives. Journal of Clinical Psychology, 59, 439–455.

Still, A., & Dryden, W. (2003). Ellis and Epictetus: Dialogue to method inpsychotherapy. *Journal of Rational - Emotive & Cognitive - BehaviorTherapy, 21*(1), 37. Retrieved September 2, 2006, from ProQuest Psychology Journals database. (Document ID: 440142401).

Still, A. (2001). Marginalisation is not unbearable. Is it even undesirable? *Journal of Rational - Emotive & Cognitive – Behavior Therapy, 19*(1), 55. Retrieved October 1, 2006, from ProQuest Psychology Journals database. (Document ID: 386245561).

Terjesen, M., DiGiuseppe, R., & Gruner, P. (2000). A review of REBT research in alcohol abuse treatment. *Journal of*

Rational - Emotive & Cognitive - Behavior Therapy: Cognitive-Behavioral Treatment of Addictions, Part I, 18(3), 165. Retrieved September 18, 2006, from ProQuest Psychology Journals database. (Document ID: 386235661).

Tiba, A. (2005). Demanding brain: Between should and shouldn't. *Journal of Cognitive & Behavioral sychotherapies, 5*(1).

Trower, P., & Jones, J. (2001). How REBT can be less disturbing and remarkably more influential in Britain: A review of views of practitioners and researchers. *Journal of Rational-Emotive & Cognitive-Behavior Therapy, 19*(1), 21-30.

Twerell, T. (1999). Presentation and defense of the use of cognitive behavioral therapy as seen in rational emotive behavioral therapy as a pastoral counseling tool http://www.nyccc.org/nyccc008.htm

Walen, S. DiGiuseppe, R. & Dryden, W. (1992). A practitioner's guide to rational-emotive therapy. New York: Springer.

Zettle, R., & Hayes, S. (1980). Conceptual and empirical status of rational-emotive therapy. *Progress in Behavior Modification, 9*, 125-166.

Ziegler, D. (2003). The concept of psychological health in rational emotive behavior therapy. *Journal of Rational-Emotive & Cognitive-Behaviour Therapy. 21*(1), 21-36.

Ziegler, D. (1999). The construct of personality in rational emotive behaviour therapy (REBT). *Journal of Rational-Emotive & Cognitive-Behaviour Therapy. 17*(1), 19-32.

Made in the USA
Lexington, KY
05 June 2012